Gretchen Bitterlin
Dennis Johnson
Donna Price
Sylvia Ramirez
K. Lynn Savage, Series Editor

# Ventures 2

## WORKBOOK

with **Deborah Gordon**

**CAMBRIDGE**
UNIVERSITY PRESS

CAMBRIDGE UNIVERSITY PRESS
Cambridge, New York, Melbourne, Madrid, Cape Town, Singapore, São Paulo, Delhi, Dubai, Tokyo, Mexico City

Cambridge University Press
32 Avenue of the Americas, New York, NY 10013–2473, USA

www.cambridge.org
Information on this title: www.cambridge.org/9780521679596

First published 2008
7th printing 2010

Printed in the United States of America

*A catalog record for this publication is available from the British Library.*

ISBN  978-0-521-54839-7 pack consisting of Student's Book and Audio CD
ISBN  978-0-521-67959-6 Workbook
ISBN  978-0-521-69080-5 pack consisting of Teacher's Edition and Teacher's Toolkit Audio CD / CD-ROM
ISBN  978-0-521-67728-8 CDs (Audio)
ISBN  978-0-521-67729-5 Cassettes
ISBN  978-0-521-67584-0 Add Ventures

*Art direction, book design, photo research, and layout services:* Adventure House, NYC

# Contents

# *Get ready*

**Personal information**

**1** Look at the picture. Write the words.

| | | | |
|---|---|---|---|
| black shoes | long black hair | short blond hair | straight hair |
| curly hair | a long skirt | a soccer uniform | striped pants |

1. *curly hair*

Alejandro

2. _____

3. _____

4. _____

5. _____

6. _____

7. _____

8. _____

Jane

Carina

Sandra

**2** Complete the sentences. Use the words from Exercise 1.

1. Alejandro has *curly hair* _____ .

2. Alejandro is wearing _____ .

3. Jane has _____ .

4. Jane is wearing _____ .

5. Carina has _____ .

6. Carina is wearing _____ on her feet.

7. Sandra has _____ .

8. Sandra is wearing _____ .

*Check your answers. See page 128.*

## 3 Write the words.

| black | blond | brown | curly | long | short | straight |

_black_ ____  ____ ____  ____ ____

**Hair color**   **Hair length**   **Hair type**

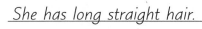
____

## 4 Look at the pictures. Write sentences. Use *long*, *short*, *straight*, and *curly*.

She has long straight hair.
_____

_____
_____

_____
_____

_____
_____

Check your answers. See page 128.

# *She's wearing a short plaid skirt.*

**1** Write the words in the correct order.

1. striped / a / green and white / dress
   *a green and white striped dress*

2. shirt / checked / black and blue / a
   _____

3. a / blue / coat / long
   _____

4. small / shoes / red and yellow
   _____

5. pants / black / plaid
   _____

6. boots / brown / short
   _____

**2** Look at the pictures. Write the words from Exercise 1.

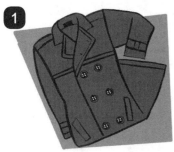  

*a long blue coat* _____ _____
_____ _____ _____

_____ _____ _____
_____ _____ _____

*Check your answers. See page 128.*

**3** Read the sentences. Look at the ad. Circle the answers.

1. Model A is wearing a _____ skirt.
   a. plaid
   b. striped
   c. checked

2. Model A has _____ hair.
   a. long curly
   b. short straight
   c. long straight

3. Model B has _____ hair.
   a. long curly
   b. short curly
   c. short straight

4. Model C is wearing a _____ shirt.
   a. plaid
   b. striped
   c. checked

5. Model D is wearing a striped _____ .
   a. sweater
   b. pants
   c. skirt

6. Model E is wearing a long _____ .
   a. sweater
   b. coat
   c. dress

**4** Write the words.

| black | green | large | pants | red | small |
|-------|-------|-------|-------|-----|-------|
| coat | jeans | long | purple | short | sweater |

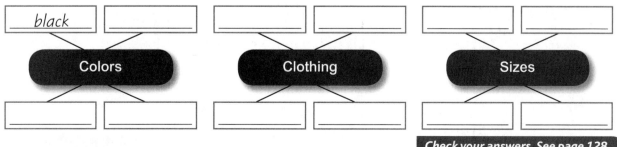

| _black_ | | | | | |
|---------|---|---|---|---|---|

Colors          Clothing          Sizes

Check your answers. See page 128.

# What are you doing right now?

*Study the chart on page 122.*

## 1 Read the questions. Circle the answers.

1. What are you doing right now?
   a. I study for a test.
   (b.) I'm studying for a test.

2. What do you usually do at night?
   a. I usually study English.
   b. I am usually studying English.

3. What do you always wear to work?
   a. I'm always wearing my uniform.
   b. I always wear my uniform.

4. What are you wearing today?
   a. I'm wearing jeans and a shirt.
   b. I wear jeans and a shirt.

5. What do you usually do on the weekend?
   a. I visit with my family.
   b. I'm visiting with my family.

6. What do you do every Tuesday?
   a. I'm going to the park.
   b. I go to the park.

## 2 Complete the conversations. Use the correct form of the verb. Use *am*, *is*, *are*, *do*, or *does*.

1. **A** What _____*do*_____ you _____*do*_____ every Thursday night?
      (do)

   **B** I _____ English.
         (study)

   **A** What _____ you _____ now?
                              (do)

   **B** I _____ a book.
            (read)

2. **A** What _____ Jin Ho _____ right now?
                                    (do)

   **B** He _____ soccer.
            (play)

   **A** What _____ Jin Ho usually _____ every day?
                                              (do)

   **B** He usually _____ computer games.
                      (play)

3. **A** What _____ Ramona _____ every afternoon?
                                    (do)

   **B** She _____ .
             (work)

   **A** What _____ Ramona _____ now?
                                    (do)

   **B** She _____ TV.
             (watch)

4. **A** What _____ Yana _____ on the weekend?
                                  (do)

   **B** She usually _____ with her family.
                       (relax)

   **A** What _____ Yana _____ now?
                                  (do)

   **B** She _____ Russian to her son.
             (teach)

*Check your answers. See page 128.*

**3** Circle the correct question.

1. He goes home.
   - (a.) What does he do at 9:00?
   - b. What is he doing right now?

2. He calls the office.
   - a. What does he do every Monday?
   - b. What is he doing now?

3. He's watching a movie.
   - a. What does he do every night?
   - b. What is he doing right now?

4. He's drinking orange juice.
   - a. What does he drink every day?
   - b. What is he drinking now?

5. He sits at his desk.
   - a. Where does he sit every night?
   - b. Where is he sitting right now?

6. He's wearing a striped suit.
   - a. What does he wear to work every day?
   - b. What is he wearing today?

**4** Complete the sentences. Use the simple present form of the verbs.

| call | drink | go | leave | sit | study | talk |
|------|-------|-----|-------|-----|-------|------|

Eduardo usually ___*leaves*___ English
              1.
class at 9:00 p.m. He _____ home
                        2.
and _____ his girlfriend, Lisa.
        3.
They usually _____ for 15 minutes.
                  4.
Then Eduardo _____ at his desk.
                   5.
He _____ coffee and _____
      6.                          7.
English late at night.

**5** Complete the sentences. Use the present continuous form of the verbs.

| drink | relax | sit | speak | watch | wear |
|-------|-------|-----|-------|-------|------|

Tonight, Eduardo ___*is relaxing*___ .
                      1.
He _____ TV with Lisa.
      2.
They _____ on the sofa.
        3.
He _____ a soda.
      4.
He _____ jeans and a shirt.
      5.
He _____ English with
      6.
Lisa. She is a good teacher!

Check your answers. See page 128.

*Reading*

**1** Read the e-mail. Complete the chart with the underlined words.

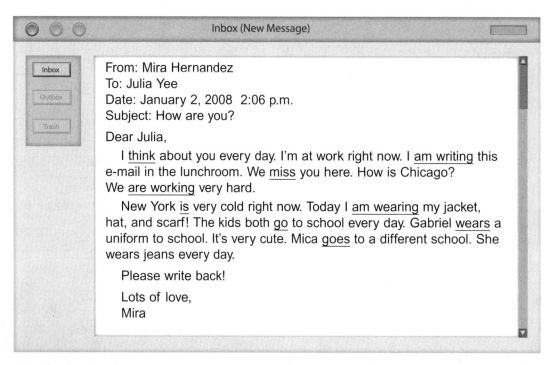

Inbox (New Message)

Inbox
Outbox
Trash

From: Mira Hernandez
To: Julia Yee
Date: January 2, 2008  2:06 p.m.
Subject: How are you?

Dear Julia,

   I <u>think</u> about you every day. I'm at work right now. I <u>am writing</u> this e-mail in the lunchroom. We <u>miss</u> you here. How is Chicago? We <u>are working</u> very hard.

   New York <u>is</u> very cold right now. Today I <u>am wearing</u> my jacket, hat, and scarf! The kids both <u>go</u> to school every day. Gabriel <u>wears</u> a uniform to school. It's very cute. Mica <u>goes</u> to a different school. She wears jeans every day.

   Please write back!

   Lots of love,
   Mira

| Present continuous | *am writing* | | |
|---|---|---|---|
| **Simple present** | *think* | | | | |

**2** Answer the questions. Use the information from Exercise 1.

1. Where is Mira right now?

   *She's at the store in the lunchroom.*

2. What city does Julia live in?

   _____

3. What city does Mira live in?

   _____

4. What does Gabriel wear to school?

   _____

5. What does Mica wear to school every day?

   _____

6. What is Mira doing right now?

   _____

**Check your answers. See page 128.**

## 3 Find the words.

bracelet
earrings
gloves
hat
necklace
purse
ring
scarf
tie
watch

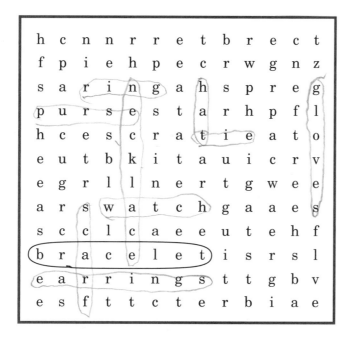

| h | c | n | n | r | r | e | t | b | r | e | c | t |
| f | p | i | e | h | p | e | c | r | w | g | n | z |
| s | a | r | i | n | g | a | h | s | p | r | e | g |
| p | u | r | s | e | s | t | a | r | h | p | f | l |
| h | c | e | s | c | r | a | t | i | e | a | t | o |
| e | u | t | b | k | i | t | a | u | i | c | r | v |
| e | g | r | l | l | n | e | r | t | g | w | e | e |
| a | r | s | w | a | t | c | h | g | a | a | e | s |
| s | c | c | l | c | a | e | e | u | t | e | h | f |
| b | r | a | c | e | l | e | t | i | s | r | s | l |
| e | a | r | r | i | n | g | s | t | t | g | b | v |
| e | s | f | t | t | c | t | e | r | b | i | a | e |

## 4 Look at the picture. Write the words from Exercise 3.

1. *earrings*

2. _____

3. _____

4. _____

5. _____

6. _____

7. _____

8. _____

9. _____

10. _____

Check your answers. See page 128.

**1** Read the chart. Complete the paragraphs.

| Name | Sarah | Martina | Norma |
|---|---|---|---|
| **Hair color** | brown | blond | black |
| **Eye color** | brown | blue | green |
| **Clothes** | red and white striped sweater, blue jeans | black shirt, black pants, red shoes | blue jacket, yellow shirt, gray plaid skirt |
| **Accessories** | scarf, hat | gold watch, red purse | large earrings, rings |
| **After-class activities** | go to work | go out with friends | go home |
| **Weekend activities** | exercise, play with children | study English, clean house | visit with family, watch children play sports |

**A**

This person has black hair and ___*green*___ eyes. She _____ home
                                    1.                         2.
every day after class. On the weekend, she _____ with her family and
                                            3.
_____ her children play sports. She is wearing a blue _____ ,
    4.                                                          5.
large _____ , and rings. Who is she? _____
       6.                                      7.

**B**

This person has _____ eyes and brown hair. She's wearing a red and
                    1.
_____ striped sweater and blue _____ . She _____ to
    2.                                   3.                   4.
work after class every day. On the weekend, she exercises and _____
                                                               5.
with her children. Who is she? _____
                                6.

**C**

Today, this person is _____ black clothing. Her _____ and
                        1.                                 2.
purse are red. She has _____ hair and _____ eyes. After class,
                        3.                     4.
she _____ out with her friends. On the weekend, she _____
      5.                                                      6.
English and cleans her house. Who is this person? _____
                                                    7.

*Check your answers. See page 129.*

**10  Unit 1**

**2** Rewrite the sentences. Change the underlined words.
Use the words in the box.

| | |
|---|---|
| a backpack | is wearing |
| every Monday | on the weekend |
| is long | a watch |

1. Bobby goes to New York City <u>every Saturday and Sunday</u>.

   *Bobby goes to New York City on the weekend.*

2. Georgia <u>is in</u> a black scarf and a red coat.

   _____

3. Susana goes to work after school <u>on Monday</u>.

   _____

4. Mei's hair <u>isn't short</u>.

   _____

5. Martin is carrying his books in <u>a bag on his back</u>.

   _____

6. Christina is wearing <u>a bracelet with a small clock on it</u>.

   _____

**3** Rewrite the sentences in a different way.

1. Mary teaches English on the weekend.

   *On the weekend, Mary teaches English.*

2. Every night, Sam leaves early.

   _____

3. On Thursday, Alberto watches TV.

   _____

4. Raquel plays volleyball on Saturday.

   _____

5. Michael wears a suit every Sunday.

   _____

6. Every June, Petra has a birthday party.

   _____

Check your answers. See page 129.

*Another view*

**1** Read the questions. Look at the ad. Circle the answers.

1. How much does the plaid shirt cost?
   a. $14.00
   b. $22.00
   c. $25.00
   d. $32.00

2. Which item costs $12.00?
   a. the necklace
   b. the ring
   c. the scarf
   d. the tie

3. When does Allene's Attic close today?
   a. 7:00 a.m.
   b. 10:00 a.m.
   c. noon
   d. midnight

4. Which item costs $62.00?
   a. the purse
   b. the boots
   c. the coat
   d. the necklace

5. How much do the pants cost?
   a. $20.00
   b. $32.00
   c. $45.00
   d. $100.00

6. Which item costs $120.00?
   a. the long boots
   b. the long coat
   c. the short skirt
   d. the striped suit

Check your answers. See page 129.

**2** Complete the puzzle.

**Across**

1.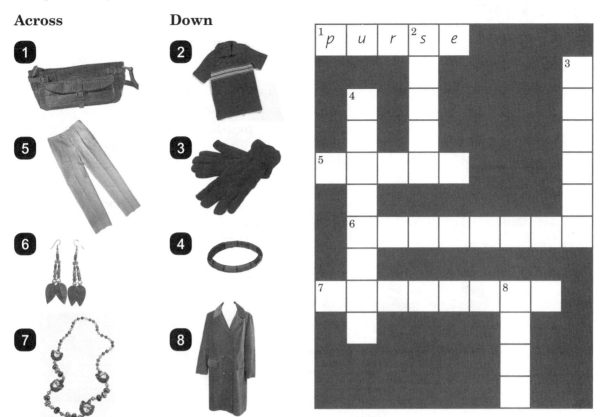
5.
6.
7.

**Down**

2.
3.
4.
8.

|   |   |   |   |   |   |   |
|---|---|---|---|---|---|---|
| ¹p | u | r | ²s | e |   |   |

**3** Write the words. Use the words from Exercise 2.

1. _____earrings_____
2. _____
3. _____
4. _____
5. _____
6. _____
7. _____

Betty's BOUTIQUE

Check your answers. See page 129.

# *Get ready*

**1** Write the words.

| | | | |
|---|---|---|---|
| a computer lab | a keyboard | a monitor | a student |
| a hall | a lab instructor | a mouse | |

1. *a computer lab*

2. _____

3. _____

4. _____

5. _____

6. _____

7. _____

**2** Complete the conversation.

| computer | instructor | keyboarding | register | skill | work |
|---|---|---|---|---|---|

**A** Hi. I need to learn _____*keyboarding*_____ .
                           1.

**B** Great. I'm Ms. Moreno. I'm the _____ . Why do
                                             2.

  you want to learn to use a _____ ?
                                            3.

**A** I need to learn for my _____ .
                                      4.

**B** That's great. Keyboarding is an important _____ .
                                               5.

  Did you _____ in the office?
                        6.

**A** Yes.

**B** OK. Have a seat, please.

*Check your answers. See page 129.*

**3** Read Diego's schedule. Answer the questions.

| Name: | Diego Sanchez | | | |
|---|---|---|---|---|
| Student ID: | 555-23-0967 | | | |
| **Class** | **Room** | **Day** | **Time** | **Teacher** |
| English | H102 | MW | 6:00–7:50 p.m. | Hilary Bowman |
| Computer lab | H315 | MW | 8:00–9:50 p.m. | Jane Moreno |

1. Who is Ms. Bowman? _Diego's English teacher._

2. Who is Ms. Moreno? _____

3. What is Diego's student ID number? _____

4. Where is the English class? _____

5. When is the English class? _____

6. What class is in room H315? _____

**4** Read the flyer. Answer the questions.

## GUNDER COLLEGE COMPUTER LAB

**New computer monitors and keyboards!**

Come to room **C23-25** and study with lab instructor **Roberto Peinado.**

Learn about keyboarding, word processing, e-mailing, and using the Internet.

Classes are **MWF 8:00 a.m.–10:00 a.m.** Register in **Room S210.**

**Registration hours:**
**Mon.–Thurs. 8:00 a.m.–8:00 p.m.**
**and Friday 8:00 a.m.–2:00 p.m. Register by 9/23.**

1. Who is Mr. Peinado? _The lab instructor._

2. What is new in the computer lab? _____

3. Where is the computer lab? _____

4. What can you learn in the computer lab? _____

5. Where can you register for computer classes? _____

6. When does registration end? _____

Check your answers. See page 129.

# What do you want to do?

*Study the chart on page 123.*

## 1 Match the wants and needs.

1. Lynn wants to fix cars. ___f___   a. He needs to take a computer class.

2. Joe wants to finish high school. __e__   b. They need to take a citizenship class.

3. I want to get a driver's license. __d__   c. She needs to get a second job.

4. Li and Matt want to become citizens. __b__   d. I need to take driving lessons.

5. Ann wants to make more money. __c__   e. He needs to take a GED class.

6. Karl wants to learn keyboarding. __a__   f. She needs to study auto mechanics.

## 2 Complete the sentences.

1. *A* Maria wants to get a driver's license.

   *B* She _____*needs to take*_____ driving lessons.
   (need / take)

2. *A* What does Jim want to do next year?

   *B* He _____ to community college.
   (want / go)

3. *A* What does Carrie want to do this year?

   *B* She _____ a second job.
   (want / get)

4. *A* What do you want to do this afternoon?

   *B* I _____ to a counselor about the GED.
   (want / talk)

5. *A* Excuse me. Do you need help?

   *B* Yes, thanks. I _____ keyboarding skills.
   (need / learn)

6. *A* Can I help you?

   *B* Yes, thank you. I _____ for a citizenship class.
   (need / register)

Check your answers. See page 129.

**3** Read the catalog. Answer the questions.

## Riverdale Adult Classes

**Do you want to fix cars?**
Auto mechanics: Mon.–Thurs.
8:00 a.m.–2:00 p.m.
Room 131

**Do you want to become a citizen?**
Citizenship: Mon.–Thurs.
6:00 p.m.–9:00 p.m.
Room 220

**Do you need to get a driver's license?**
Driver education: Mon.–Fri.
2:00 p.m.–4:00 p.m. by appointment
Outside in the parking lot

**Do you need to learn computer skills?**
Computer technology: Mon. & Wed.
9:00 a.m.–11:00 a.m. or
Tues. & Thurs. 1:00 p.m.–3:00 p.m.
In the computer lab

Do you want to go to college? See our counselors in Room 231.

1. **A** Carlos wants to fix cars. What class does he need to take?

   **B** *He needs to take an auto mechanics class.*

2. **A** My mother needs to get a driver's license. What class does she need to take?

   **B** _____

3. **A** My wife and I want to become citizens. What class do we need to take?

   **B** _____

4. **A** Arthur is taking an auto mechanics class. What room does he need to go to?

   **B** _____

5. **A** You want to go to college. What room do you need to go to?

   **B** _____

6. **A** My sisters want to learn computer skills. What class do they need to take?

   **B** _____

Check your answers. See page 129.

## Lesson C — What will you do?

**Lesson C**

# What will you do?

*Study the chart on page 125.*

**1** Complete the sentences. Use *will* or *won't*.

1. Javier needs to get a driver's license. He ___will___ take driving lessons next month.

2. Sally wants to make more money. She ___will___ take a vocational course.

3. Abram wants to be an auto mechanic. He ___won't___ take a citizenship class.

4. Amelia needs to learn a new language. She _____ register for a class next week.

5. Min has a test tomorrow. She ___won't___ go to the party tonight.

6. Micah needs to open a business. He ___will___ start business school soon.

**2** Read James's calendar. Answer the questions.

## James's Calendar

| Monday | Tuesday | Wednesday | Thursday | Friday | Saturday | Sunday |
|---|---|---|---|---|---|---|
| take an English class | take a driving lesson | take an English class | work | work | meet Lisa for lunch | call Mom |

1. What will James do on Thursday?

   *He'll work on Thursday.*

2. What will he do on Tuesday?

   _____

3. What will he do on Friday?

   _____

4. What will he do on Saturday?

   _____

5. What will he do on Sunday?

   _____

6. What will he do on Monday and Wednesday?

   _____

**Check your answers. See page 129.**

**3** Look at the pictures. Complete the sentences.

## Suk Jin's Plan

This year: go to the U.S.

Next year: study English

In two years: get a GED

In three years: study auto mechanics

In four years: open a business

In five years: buy a house

1. **A** What will Suk Jin do in five years?

   **B** He'll probably _buy a house_ .

2. **A** What will he do this year?

   **B** He'll probably _____ .

3. **A** What will he do in four years?

   **B** He'll most likely _____ .

4. **A** What will he do next year?

   **B** Maybe he'll _____ .

5. **A** What will he do in two years?

   **B** He'll probably _____ .

6. **A** What will he do in three years?

   **B** He'll most likely _____ .

**4** Write questions.

1. What / she / in five years _What will she do in five years?_

2. What / he / next year _____

3. What / you / tomorrow _____

4. What / they / this weekend _____

5. What / you / in two years _____

6. What / we / tonight _____

*Check your answers. See page 129.*

# Lesson D Reading

**1** Read the ad. Answer the questions.

## Learn Computer Technology at City College

Get a job as a computer technician in 18 months! No time?
Don't worry. All courses are at night and on weekends.

*There will be an information session on March 14 at 7:30 at City College.*

We'll talk about registration, the classes, and the certificate.
Come and ask questions! Teachers and current students
will be there.

1. How long is the Computer Technology program? _18 months._____

2. When is the information session? _____

3. Where is the information session? _____

4. What will they discuss at the information session? _____

   _____

5. Who will be there from the school? _____

**2** Read about Megan's goal. Circle the answers.

> ## My Goal
>
>    I want to open my own coffee shop. I need to take three steps. First, I need to take business classes. Second, I need to get a job in a coffee shop. Third, I need to learn about the coffee-shop business. I think I can reach my goal in three years.

1. Megan wants to _____ .
   a. become a citizen
   b. open a coffee shop
   c. finish high school

2. First, she needs to _____ .
   a. get her GED
   b. get a job
   c. take business classes

3. Second, she needs to _____ .
   a. learn about the coffee-shop business
   b. open her coffee shop
   c. get a job in a coffee shop

4. In three years, Megan will probably _____ .
   a. open her coffee shop
   b. get a job in a dress shop
   c. finish business school

*Check your answers. See page 130.*

**3** Match the names of the vocational courses.

1. computer  _e_      a. arts
2. automotive ____     b. design
3. culinary ____       c. management
4. home health ____    d. repair
5. hotel ____          e. technology
6. landscape ____      f. care

**4** Look at the pictures. Write the vocational courses.

| | | | |
|---|---|---|---|
| accounting | computer technology | home health care | landscape design |
| automotive repair | culinary arts | hotel management | nursing |

# Study at Peterson Vocational School!

## We offer:

**1**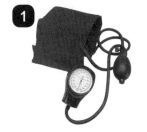

___nursing___

**2**

_____

**3**

_____

**4**

_____

**5**

_____

**6**

_____

**7**

_____

**8**

_____

Check your answers. See page 130.

**1** Match the goals with the steps.

**Goals**

1. Pablo wants to finish high school. _*b*_

2. Elena wants to learn keyboarding. ____

3. Jeff wants to learn how to fix cars. ____

4. They want to study hotel management. ____

5. Marina wants to become a citizen. ____

6. Toan wants to speak and understand English. ____

**Steps needed to reach the goals**

a. They need to take hotel management classes.

b. He needs to take the GED test.

c. She needs to learn to write in English.

d. She needs to take a computer class.

e. He needs to make English-speaking friends.

f. He needs to take an automotive repair class.

**2** Read about Quan's goal. Complete the sentences.

## My Goal for Next Year

I have a new goal for next year. I want to get a second job on the weekend. I need to make more money because we have a new baby. I will take three steps to reach my goal. First, I need to talk to people about job possibilities. Second, I need to read the classified section of the newspaper. Third, I need to look for jobs online. I will probably reach my goal in two months.

1. Quan wants to _get a second job on the weekend_____ .

2. He needs more money because _____ .

3. First, he needs to _____ .

4. Second, he needs to _____ .

5. Third, he needs to _____ .

6. He will probably reach his goal in _two month_____ .

Check your answers. See page 130.

**3** Complete the sentences.

| children | First | goal | Second | Third | year |
|----------|-------|------|--------|-------|------|

### Rachel's Goal

Rachel has a big ___*goal*___ . She wants
1.

to help her _____ with their homework.
2.

_____ , she needs to find an adult school.
3.

_____ , she needs to practice her English
4.

every day. _____ , she needs to volunteer
5.

with the Parent-Teacher Association (PTA) at her

children's school. She'll probably be ready to

help her children next _____ .
6.

**4** Answer the questions. Use the story in Exercise 3.

1. What is Rachel's goal?

   *She wants to help her children with their homework.*

2. What does Rachel need to do first?

   _____

3. What does Rachel need to do second?

   _____

4. What does Rachel need to do third?

   _____

5. When will Rachel be ready to help her children?

   _____

*Check your answers. See page 130.*

**1** Read the questions. Look at the college catalog. Circle the answers.

## ORANGE COUNTY COMMUNITY COLLEGE

| Catalog page | Courses | Spring | Summer | Fall |
|---|---|---|---|---|
| 51 | Accounting | 📖 | | |
| 52 | Culinary Arts | 🏠 | 📖 | |
| 52 | Advanced Landscape Design | 🏠 | | 📖 |
| 53 | Counseling 1 | | 🏠 | 📖 |
| 54 | Beginning Hotel Management | 🏠 | | 🏠 |

📖 City Downtown Library      🏠 City Community Center

1. The classes meet in ____ .
   a. one place
   (b.) two places
   c. three places
   d. four places

2. There will be only two courses in the ____ .
   a. fall
   b. winter
   c. spring
   d. summer

3. Classes in ____ are only at the City Downtown Library.
   a. Accounting
   b. Beginning Hotel Management
   c. Counseling 1
   d. Culinary Arts

4. Counseling 1 is on catalog page ____ .
   a. 51
   b. 52
   c. 53
   d. 54

5. Students can take ____ in the summer.
   a. Accounting
   b. Advanced Landscape Design
   c. Beginning Hotel Management
   d. Culinary Arts

6. There will be ____ classes in Beginning Hotel Management.
   a. one
   b. two
   c. three
   d. four

*Check your answers. See page 130.*

# 2 Write the words. Complete the puzzle.

## Down

**1**

_____culinary_____ arts

**2**

_____ management

**3**

_____ design

**4**

_____ health care

**5**

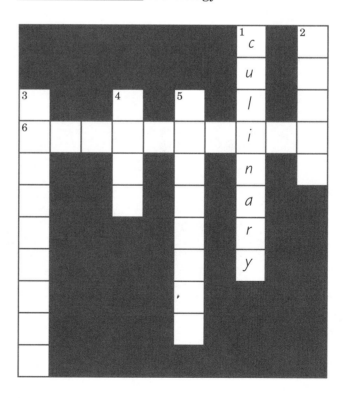

_____ technology

## Across

**6**

_____ repair

|   |   |   |   |   | 1 c |   | 2 |
|---|---|---|---|---|-----|---|---|
|   |   |   |   |   | u   |   |   |
| 3 |   | 4 |   | 5 | l   |   |   |
| 6 |   |   |   |   | i   |   |   |
|   |   |   |   |   | n   |   |   |
|   |   |   |   |   | a   |   |   |
|   |   |   |   |   | r   |   |   |
|   |   |   |   |   | y   |   |   |
|   |   |   |   |   |     |   |   |
|   |   |   |   |   |     |   |   |
|   |   |   |   |   |     |   |   |

Check your answers. See page 130.

## Lesson **A** Get ready

**1** Complete the words.

1. s m <u>o</u> k <u>e</u>
2. g r __ c __ r __ __ s
3. s __ p __ r m __ r k __ t
4. e __ __ i n __
5. b r __ __ k __ n - d __ __ w n  c __ r
6. c __ l l  p h __ n __
7. t r __ n k
8. __ o o __

**2** Write the words from Exercise 1.

4. _____
5. _____
1. _____
2. _____
6. _____
3. _____
7. _____
8. _____

*Check your answers. See page 130.*

**3** Look at the picture. Complete the conversation.

| broke | engine | groceries | hood | smoke | supermarket | trunk |

**A** Hi Miguel.

**B** Laurie? Are you OK?

**A** Yes. But the car _____*broke*_____ down.
1.

**B** Where are you?

**A** We're near the _____ . I bought a lot of _____ .
2.                                              3.

I put them in the _____ . Then I started the car, but
4.

_____ came from the _____ .
5.                                         6.

**B** Did you open the _____ ?
7.

**A** Yes. I called the mechanic, too.

**B** OK. I'll be right there.

*Check your answers. See page 130.*

**Friends and family 27**

# What did you do last weekend?

*Study the chart on page 124.*

**1** Look at the picture and read the e-mail. Circle the answers.

From: shin17@cup.org
To: grandma17@cup.org
Date: August 10, 2008
Subject: Picnic last week

Here's a picture from last weekend! We had a great time.

Love,
Shin

1. What did Shin do last weekend?
   a. He went to the beach.
   b. He went to the park.

2. Did he take his children?
   a. Yes, he did.
   b. No, he didn't.

3. Did he take the bus?
   a. Yes, he did.
   b. No, he didn't.

4. Did he barbecue hamburgers?
   a. Yes, he did.
   b. No, he didn't.

5. What did his son do?
   a. He read a book.
   b. He listened to music.

6. Did his daughter listen to music?
   a. Yes, she did.
   b. No, she didn't.

**2** Write the simple past.

1. barbecue    *barbecued*
2. buy    _____
3. drive    _____
4. eat    _____
5. fix    _____
6. go    _____

7. have    _____
8. listen    _____
9. meet    _____
10. play    _____
11. read    _____
12. stay    _____

Check your answers. See page 130.

**3** Complete the sentences. Use the simple past.

1. Frankie and Claudia ___*went*___ to the park.
   (go)
2. They _____ their friends.
   (meet)
3. They _____ soccer.
   (play)
4. They _____ a picnic dinner.
   (have)
5. They _____ birthday cake.
   (eat)
6. They _____ home.
   (drive)

**4** Match the pictures with the sentences in Exercise 3.

a. __5__

b. _____

c. _____

d. _____

e. _____

f. _____

Check your answers. See page 130.

# *When do you usually play soccer?*

*Study the chart on page 124.*

**1** Complete the sentences. Use the simple present or the simple past.

1. Anton _____ *went* _____ to English class at 7:00 last night.
   (go)

2. Mom and Dad usually _____ my soccer game on Thursday.
   (watch)

3. Anita _____ her apartment last Saturday.
   (clean)

4. Tom usually _____ dinner at home.
   (eat)

5. I usually _____ for work at 8:15 a.m.
   (leave)

6. Adriana _____ her friends after class yesterday.
   (meet)

**2** Read Malik's datebook from last week. Match the questions with the answers.

| Sunday | *get up late!* |
|---|---|
| Monday | *work → 5:00* |
| | ~~*tennis with Geraldo 6:00 p.m.*~~ |
| Tuesday | *8:00 ESL class before work* |
| | *work → 5:00* |
| Wednesday | *work → 5:00* |
| | *Reza's soccer game 5:30* |
| Thursday | *8:00 ESL class* |
| | *work → 5:00* |
| | *birthday dinner at Mom and Dad's at 7:00* |
| Friday | *leave work early* |
| | *citizenship class at 4:00* |
| Saturday | *tennis with Geraldo 9:00 a.m.* |

1. When does Malik usually finish work? _*d*_        a. Tuesday and Thursday.

2. What day did Malik finish work early last week? _____        b. On Sunday.

3. What did Malik have at 4:00 on Friday? _____        c. At his parents' house.

4. When did Malik sleep late? _____        d. At 5:00.

5. Did Malik play tennis with Geraldo on Monday? _____        e. A citizenship class.

6. Where did Malik eat dinner last Thursday? _____        f. No, he didn't.

7. What days does Malik have ESL class? _____        g. On Friday.

8. What day did Malik watch Reza's soccer game? _____        h. On Wednesday.

*Check your answers. See page 130.*

**3** Complete the sentences. Use the simple present or the simple past.

1. Malik _____has_____ ESL class on Tuesday and Thursday.
   (have)

2. Malik usually _____ tennis with Geraldo on Monday
   (play)
   and Saturday.

3. Malik usually _____ until 5:00.
   (work)

4. Malik _____ a citizenship class every Friday at 4:00.
   (have)

5. Malik and Geraldo _____ for tennis at 9:00 last Saturday morning.
   (meet)

6. Malik usually _____ up late on Sunday.
   (get)

7. Malik and his wife and children usually _____ dinner at home.
   (eat)

8. They _____ dinner at his parents' house last Thursday.
   (eat)

**4** Read the Lopez family's calendar. Answer the questions.

| Monday | Tuesday | Wednesday | Thursday | Friday |
|--------|---------|-----------|----------|--------|
| Melissa – movie with Uncle Jaime | Tony – meet friends after work 6:00 | Victor – study for English test | Mom and Dad – buy groceries | Mom – take English exam<br><br>Tony – meet friends after work 5:30 |

1. When do Mom and Dad usually buy groceries?

   _They usually buy groceries on Thursday._

2. When did Mom take her English exam?

   _____

3. What does Tony usually do on Tuesday and Friday?

   _____

4. When did Melissa go to a movie with her uncle?

   _____

5. What time did Tony meet his friends last Friday?

   _____

6. What did Victor do last Wednesday?

   _____

Check your answers. See page 130.

## Lesson D Reading

**1** Read Ana's journal. Answer the questions.

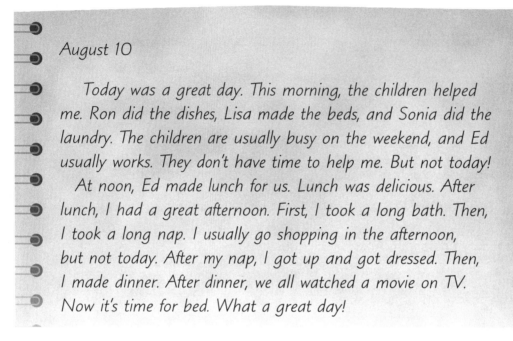

*August 10*

    *Today was a great day. This morning, the children helped me. Ron did the dishes, Lisa made the beds, and Sonia did the laundry. The children are usually busy on the weekend, and Ed usually works. They don't have time to help me. But not today!*
    *At noon, Ed made lunch for us. Lunch was delicious. After lunch, I had a great afternoon. First, I took a long bath. Then, I took a long nap. I usually go shopping in the afternoon, but not today. After my nap, I got up and got dressed. Then, I made dinner. After dinner, we all watched a movie on TV. Now it's time for bed. What a great day!*

1. Who helped Ana today?
   a. Ron
   b. Lisa
   c. Sonia
   (d.) all of the above

2. Who did the dishes?
   a. Ed
   b. Lisa
   c. Ron
   d. Sonia

3. Who made the beds?
   a. Ed
   b. Lisa
   c. Ron
   d. Sonia

4. Who did the laundry?
   a. Ed
   b. Lisa
   c. Ron
   d. Sonia

5. Who made lunch?
   a. Ed
   b. Lisa
   c. Ron
   d. Sonia

6. Who usually helps Ana?
   a. Ana's friends
   b. the children
   c. Ed
   d. none of the above

7. Who took a long bath and a long nap?
   a. Ana
   b. the children
   c. Ed
   d. all of the above

8. Who made dinner?
   a. Ana
   b. the children
   c. Ed
   d. all of the above

*Check your answers. See page 130.*

**2** Complete the chart.

| a bath | the bed | the dishes | dressed | the laundry | lunch | a nap | up |
|--------|---------|------------|---------|-------------|-------|-------|-----|

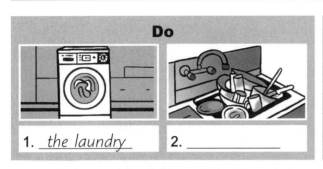

**Do**

1. _the laundry_

2. _____

**Make**

3. _____

4. _____

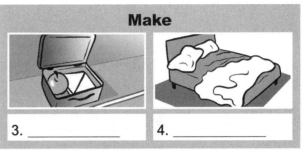

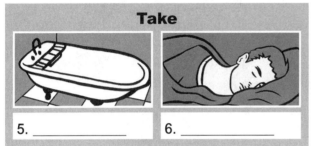

**Take**

5. _____

6. _____

**Get**

7. _____

8. _____

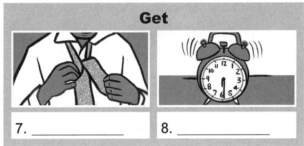

**3** Read the conversation. Write *do*, *make*, or *take*. Use the simple present or the simple past.

1. **Mom** Sonia, did you __make__ the beds this morning?

2. **Sonia** No, I didn't, Mom. But I always _____ the beds. It's Ron's turn.

3. **Ron** Mom, I can't make the beds. I don't have time. And I always _____

   the dishes. It's Lisa's turn.

   **Lisa** OK, Mom. In a minute.

4. **Mom** Ron, did you _____ the dishes this morning?

5. **Ron** Yes, I _____ .

   **Mom** And what about your homework?

6. **Ron** I _____ my homework yesterday. Today is Saturday.

7. **Mom** OK. Did Dad _____ the laundry this morning?

8. **Sonia** No, Mom. He always _____ a nap on Saturday.

   **Mom** A nap! It's 9:00 a.m.

Check your answers. See page 131.

**1** Read Ana's schedule. Look at the picture. Answer the questions.

*Usually*

*This morning*

**My Morning Schedule**
6:00: *Get up and take a bath.*
6:15: *Get Ed up and then get dressed.*
6:30: *Get Sonia up and then make the children's lunches for school.*
6:45: *Get Ron up and then make my lunch.*
7:10: *Get Lisa up and then eat my breakfast.*
7:15: *Check the children's beds.*
7:20: *Ed leaves for work.*
7:30: *Children leave for school.*
7:45: *Do the dishes.*
7:55: *Leave for work.*

Ana

Ron

1. Who usually gets up first?

   *Ana usually gets up first.*

2. Who got up first this morning?

   _____

3. Who usually gets the family up?

   _____

4. Who got Ana up this morning?

   _____

5. Who usually takes a bath every morning?

   _____

6. Who didn't take a bath this morning?

   _____

7. Who usually leaves for work at 7:20?

   _____

**Check your answers. See page 131.**

**2** Answer the questions. Use Ana's schedule in Exercise 1.

1. When does Ana get dressed?  _She gets dressed at 6:15._

2. When does Ana get Sonia up?  _____

3. When does Ana eat her breakfast?  _____

4. When does Ana do the dishes?  _____

5. When does Ana check the children's beds?  _____

_____

6. When does Ana leave the house?  _____

**3** Read the sentences. Write *First*, *Next*, or *Finally* on the correct line.

1. Last Monday, I had a very bad morning.

_____ , I didn't have time for breakfast.

____*First*____ , I woke up late.

_____ , I was late for work.

2. Last Sunday, my family went to the beach.

_____ , we drove home for dinner.

_____ , we had a picnic lunch.

_____ , we relaxed all afternoon.

**4** Write the sentences from Exercise 3 in the correct order.

1. _Last Monday, I had a very bad morning. First, I woke up late. Next,_ _____

_____

_____

2. _____

_____

_____

Check your answers. See page 131.

# Another view

**1** Read the questions. Look at the ad. Circle the answers.

JACKSON REPAIR

Next to the supermarket on Washington Street   (973) 555-1850

- We fix car problems from hood to trunk!
- SUMMER REPAIR SPECIAL: 20% off!
- ENGINE SPECIAL: $150
- BROKEN-DOWN CAR?
  We'll bring you home! $50

OPEN MONDAY–SATURDAY 8:00 a.m.– 6:00 p.m.

1. How much is the engine special?
   a. $50
   b. $100
   c. $150
   d. $200

2. What is the Jackson Repair phone number?
   a. 20%
   b. $50
   c. $150
   d. (973) 555-1850

3. What is the Summer Repair Special?
   a. 20% off
   b. $50 off
   c. 50% off
   d. $150 off

4. Which days is Jackson Repair open?
   a. Monday–Friday
   b. Monday–Saturday
   c. Monday–Sunday
   d. Sunday–Saturday

5. When is Jackson Repair open?
   a. 6:00 a.m.–8:00 p.m.
   b. 6:00 p.m.–8:00 p.m.
   c. 8:00 a.m.–6:00 p.m.
   d. 8:00 p.m.–6:00 a.m.

6. Where is Jackson Repair?
   a. at home
   b. on Jackson Street
   c. in the supermarket
   d. on Washington Street

Check your answers. See page 131.

**2** Look at the pictures. Complete the sentences.

1. (play, volleyball / soccer) Max usually _____*plays volleyball*_____ .
   Last night, he _____*played soccer*_____ .

2. (go, to the movies / to the mall) Susie usually
   _____ on Saturday. Last Saturday,
   she _____ .

3. (barbecue, chicken / hamburgers) The Smiths
   usually _____ . Yesterday, they
   _____ .

4. (drive, to the beach / to the mountains) On the weekend,
   Lin usually _____ . Last weekend,
   she _____ .

5. (clean, her apartment / her car) On Sunday, Maisie
   usually _____ . Last Sunday,
   she _____ .

**3** Find the words.

| dishes |
| dressed |
| homework |
| laundry |
| make |
| morning |
| take |
| yesterday |

| d | l | n | o | r | e | k | r | g | s | m | m |
|---|---|---|---|---|---|---|---|---|---|---|---|
| s | l | a | u | n | d | r | y | m | m | d | a |
| h | l | o | d | h | o | m | e | w | o | r | k |
| y | e | d | i | s | h | e | s | y | r | e | e |
| m | d | g | n | e | z | r | t | u | n | s | k |
| i | t | o | u | s | o | o | e | h | i | s | a |
| y | d | m | d | o | e | n | r | h | n | e | k |
| r | k | e | s | r | e | n | d | k | g | d | e |
| a | s | n | e | e | s | t | a | k | e | s | k |
| s | n | e | n | a | s | d | y | k | i | o | e |
| a | d | o | m | y | h | e | r | s | m | t | s |

Check your answers. See page 131.

# Get ready

**Health**

## 1 Complete the words.

1. h _a_ n d
2. c r __ t c h __ s
3. __ c c __ d __ n t
4. m __ d __ c __ n __
5. l __ g
6. h __ __ d __ c h __
7. X - r __ __
8. h __ s p __ t __ l

## 2 Look at the picture. Write the words from Exercise 1.

1. _____ hospital _____
2. _____
3. _____
4. _____
5. _____
6. _____
7. _____
8. _____

*Check your answers. See page 131.*

## 3 Find the words.

| accident |
| crutches |
| headache |
| hospital |
| hurt |
| medicine |
| X-ray |

| s | h | e | h | c | a | a | o | r | h | r |
|---|---|---|---|---|---|---|---|---|---|---|
| e | c | e | h | u | r | d | r | s | h | n |
| h | r | a | a | c | i | s | h | i | a | t |
| x | u | c | s | c | e | n | u | n | c | e |
| r | t | i | e | e | n | e | r | d | r | p |
| a | c | c | i | d | e | n | t | x | r | d |
| y | h | e | a | d | a | c | h | e | i | e |
| m | e | d | i | c | i | n | e | n | u | h |
| t | s | h | o | s | p | i | t | a | l | o |
| e | h | s | t | h | c | i | a | h | n | e |
| a | e | i | c | m | i | h | s | t | e | c |

## 4 Complete the sentences. Use the words from Exercise 3.

1. John had an _____accident_____ at work.

2. He _____ his knee.

3. He went to the _____ .

4. The doctor took an _____ of his knee.

5. John had to walk with _____ .

6. He took _____ for the pain.

7. He also had a _____ .

## 5 Look at the pictures. Write sentences. Use *hurt*.

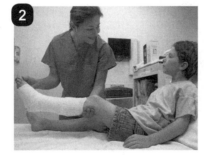

*She hurt her arm.*  _____  _____

_____  _____  _____

Check your answers. See page 131.

# *What do I have to do?*

*Study the chart on page 123.*

## 1 Complete the conversations. Use *have to* or *has to*, and *do* or *does*.

1. **A** Linda hurt her hand. What ___does___ she ___have to___ do?

   **B** She ___has to___ see a doctor.

2. **A** Rod hurt his back. What ___dec s___ he ___have to___ do?

   **B** He ___has to___ stay home today.

3. **A** Jimmy broke his arm. What ___do___ we _____ do?

   **B** We _____ take Jimmy to the hospital.

4. **A** I have a headache. What _____ I _____ do?

   **B** You _____ go home early.

5. **A** Tim broke his leg. What _____ he _____ do?

   **B** He _____ use these crutches.

6. **A** Jerry and Charlie have asthma. What _____ they _____ do?

   **B** They _____ take their medicine.

## 2 Answer the questions. Use *have to* or *has to*.

1. Jesse sprained his ankle. What does he have to do?

   (use crutches) *He has to use crutches.*

2. Mari burned her hand. What does she have to do?

   (see the doctor) _____

3. Irvin broke his arm. What does he have to do?

   (get an X-ray) _____

4. Elian hurt his hand at work. What does he have to do?

   (fill out an accident report) _____

5. Rosa has a headache. What does she have to do?

   (take medicine) _____

6. Andrea and Steve had a car accident. What do they have to do?

   (go to the hospital) _____

Check your answers. See page 131.

## 3 Match the phrases with labels.

1. You have to take this in the morning. __c__

2. You have to keep this in the refrigerator. ____

3. You have to eat when you take this. ____

4. You have to use this at night. ____

5. You have to keep this out of the refrigerator. ____

6. You have to use this in your eye. ____

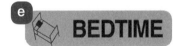

## 4 Complete the conversation.

do
food
have to
medicine
morning
prescription
refrigerator

**A** Here's your ___prescription___ , Mrs. Lopez.
                        1.

**B** Thanks. What _____ I have to do?
                        2.

**A** You _____ keep this _____ in the _____ .
              3.                           4.                          5.

**B** OK. Can I take it in the _____ ?
                                      6.

**A** Yes, and you have to take it with _____ .
                                                7.

**B** I see. I'll take it with my breakfast. Thank you, Dr. Simmons.

Check your answers. See page 131.

*Study the chart on page 125.*

**1** Circle *should* or *shouldn't*.

1. Karl's tooth hurts. He (**should**)/ **shouldn't** go to the dentist.

2. The children are all sick. They **should** / **shouldn't** go to school today.

3. My eyes hurt. I **should** / **shouldn't** watch TV right now.

4. Your leg is very sore. You **should** / **shouldn't** get an X-ray.

5. Mario hurt his back. He **should** / **shouldn't** see a doctor.

6. Alissa has a stomachache. She **should** / **shouldn't** eat a big dinner.

**2** Complete the sentences. Use *should* or *shouldn't*.

1. **A** Uncle Pete has a bottle of medicine.

   **B** He ____*shouldn't*____ freeze it.

   He ____*should*____ keep it away from children.

2. **A** Sue has a headache.

   **B** She _____ listen to loud music.

   She _____ take some aspirin.

3. **A** Abel has a stomachache.

   **B** He _____ take some medicine.

   He _____ eat his lunch.

4. **A** Francine has a sprained ankle.

   **B** She _____ play soccer.

   She _____ get a pair of crutches.

5. **A** I'm very hot. I don't feel well.

   **B** You _____ drink lots of water.

   You _____ stay in the sun.

6. **A** Mrs. Lam hurt her leg.

   **B** She _____ see a doctor.

   She _____ walk.

*Check your answers. See page 131.*

**3** Complete the sentences.

| accident | asthma | headache | medicine | sprained ankle | stomachache |
|---|---|---|---|---|---|

1. **A** I have a _sprained ankle_ .

   **B** You should use crutches.

2. **A** Alex had an _____ at work.

   **B** He should fill out an accident report.

3. **A** Carla has a _____ .

   **B** She shouldn't listen to loud music.

4. **A** Shufen has some _____ .

   **B** She should keep it in the refrigerator.

5. **A** Benjamin has a _____ .

   **B** He shouldn't eat lunch right now.

6. **A** Peter has _____ .

   **B** He should take his medicine.

**4** Complete the sentences. Use *should* or *shouldn't*.

# THE FLU

What should you do? • What shouldn't you do?

○ 1. You _____should_____ see your doctor.

○ 2. You _____ work.

○ 3. You _____ rest.

○ 4. You _____ take medicine.

○ 5. You _____ drink lots of water.

○ 6. You _____ go out.

*Check your answers. See page 132.*

# Reading

**1** Read the questions. Look at the poster. Circle the answers.

## KNOW YOUR BLOOD PRESSURE

Are you over 21? Yes? Your doctor should check your blood pressure every year. High blood pressure can be dangerous. Here are some ways to lower your blood pressure. First, try to change your lifestyle:

- Stop smoking.
- Lose weight.
- Exercise every day.
- Eat lots of fruits and vegetables. Don't eat a lot of fat.
- Don't use a lot of salt. Don't drink a lot of coffee.
- Reduce your stress.

Second, talk to your doctor about your blood pressure. Maybe you need to take medicine. Talk to your doctor! Start today!

1. What should you do to lower your blood pressure?
   a. change your lifestyle
   b. drink coffee
   c. eat fat
   d. use salt

2. You have high blood pressure. What should you eat?
   a. fat
   b. fruits
   c. salt
   d. none of the above

3. You need to lower your blood pressure. What should you do?
   a. drink coffee
   b. start smoking
   c. eat healthy foods
   d. use salt

4. You need to change your diet. What should you do?
   a. drink coffee
   b. eat vegetables
   c. exercise
   d. take medicine

5. You need to lose weight. When should you exercise?
   a. every year
   b. every month
   c. every week
   d. every day

6. Who should check your blood pressure?
   a. your doctor
   b. your English teacher
   c. your parents
   d. none of the above

Check your answers. See page 132.

## 2 Match the words.

1. a swollen  _d_       a. neck
2. high blood  ____      b. wrist
3. a sprained  ____      c. pains
4. a stiff  ____         d. knee
5. chest  ____           e. pressure

## 3 Look at the pictures. Write sentences. Use *has* or *have*.

She has a rash. _____     _____     _____

_____            _____     _____

_____            _____     _____

_____            _____     _____

## 4 Complete the sentences.

accident
chest
cut
hurt
medicine

- Did someone get ___*hurt*___ ?
  1.
- Was there a bad _____ ?
  2.
- Does someone have _____ pains?
  3.
- Does someone have a bad _____ ?
  4.
- Did a child take your _____ ?
  5.

# EMERGENCY? CALL 911

Check your answers. See page 132.

# *Writing*

**1** Read the questions. Look at the form. Answer the questions.

| Sleepy Burgers: Accident Log | | | | August 2008 |
|---|---|---|---|---|
| **Employee** | **Job** | **Date** | **Where** | **Injury** |
| J. Haddan | Waiter | 8-3-07 | Dining Room | Sprained ankle |
| M. Almaleh | Cook | 8-10-07 | Kitchen | Burned hand |
| F. Engels | Cook | 8-12-07 | Kitchen | Cut hand |
| E. Perry | Hostess | 8-20-07 | Dining Room | Sprained wrist |
| *Problems? Call the U.S. Department of Labor at (800) 555-0810.* | | | | |

1. How many accidents were there at the restaurant in August?

   *There were four accidents in August.*

2. Who had a sprained ankle?

   _____

3. When did the cook burn his hand?

   _____

4. What did Mr. Engels cut?

   _____

5. What was Ms. Perry's injury?

   _____

6. What is the name of the restaurant?

   _____

**2** Number the sentences in the correct order.

1. Yesterday, I cut my hand.

   ____ The knife slipped.

   _1_ I was cooking dinner.

   ____ My hands were wet.

2. Yesterday, I burned my leg.

   ____ My son ran into the table.

   ____ I was eating hot soup.

   ____ The table fell over.

Check your answers. See page 132.

**3** Complete the sentences.

| | | | |
|---|---|---|---|
| accident | days | injuries | shouldn't |
| burned | has to | medicine | work |

**Cottage Hospital**

**Report**

I treated Carlos Garcia today, 5/09/2007, for ___*burned*___ hands.
1.
He got these _____ at work at Fast Frank's Restaurant
2.
this afternoon. He says it was an _____ .
3.

**Recommendations**

1. Carlos _____ take one ounce of this _____
4.                                                                          5.
   every four hours for ten _____ .
6.
2. Carlos _____ work for one week. He can return
7.
   to _____ on May 16, 2007.
8.

**Signature** *William Crawford*

**Date** *May 9, 2007*

**4** Answer the questions. Use the report in Exercise 3.

1. Who was hurt?

   *Carlos Garcia was hurt.*

2. What was his injury?

   _____

3. When was he hurt?

   _____

4. Was it an accident?

   _____

5. When can he return to work?

   _____

6. What is the name of the restaurant?

   _____

Check your answers. See page 132.

# *Another view*

**1** Read the questions. Look at the bar graph. Circle the answers.

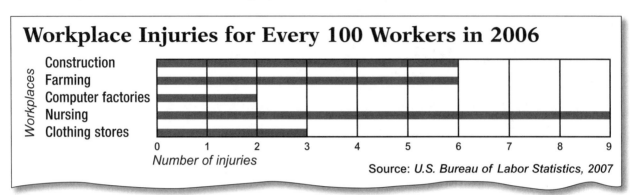

**Workplace Injuries for Every 100 Workers in 2006**

*Workplaces:* Construction, Farming, Computer factories, Nursing, Clothing stores

*Number of injuries* — Source: *U.S. Bureau of Labor Statistics, 2007*

1. What year is this bar graph for?
   a. 2004
   b. 2005
   c. 2006
   d. 2007

2. For every 100 workers, which workplace had nine injuries?
   a. construction
   b. farming
   c. nursing
   d. clothing stores

3. For every 100 workers, which workplace had two injuries?
   a. farming
   b. nursing
   c. clothing stores
   d. computer factories

4. For every 100 workers, how many injuries happened on farms?
   a. 2
   b. 3
   c. 6
   d. 9

5. For every 100 workers, how many injuries happened in clothing stores?
   a. 2
   b. 3
   c. 6
   d. 9

6. Which workplaces had the same number of injuries?
   a. farming and construction
   b. clothing stores and farming
   c. construction and nursing
   d. nursing and farming

**2** Complete the sentences.

| doctor | drowsiness | product | tablets |
|---|---|---|---|

1. Do not take more than 8 _____*tablets*_____ in 24 hours.

2. Ask a _____ before use if you have liver or kidney disease.

3. When using this _____ , do not take more than directed.

4. This medicine can cause _____ .

*Check your answers. See page 132.*

# 3 Complete the puzzle.

### Across

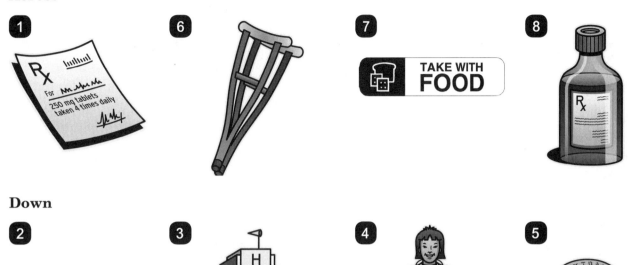

**1** **6** **7** TAKE WITH **FOOD** **8**

### Down

**2** Paul Jenkins, MD
Dr. Paul Jenkins

**3** **4** **5**

Check your answers. See page 132.

# Lesson A  *Get ready*

## 1  Complete the words.

1. a  s <u>u</u> <u>i</u> t c <u>a</u> s <u>e</u>

2. an  ___ n f ___ r m ___ t ___ ___ n  d ___ s k

3. a  w ___ ___ t ___ n g  ___ r ___ ___

4. a  t r ___ c k  n ___ m b ___ r

5. a  t ___ c k ___ t  b ___ ___ ___ t h

6. a  d ___ p ___ r t ___ r ___  b ___ ___ r d

## 2  Look at the picture. Write the words from Exercise 1.

**1.** _a ticket booth_

**4.** _____

**2.** _____

**5.** _____

**3.** _____

**6.** _____

*Check your answers. See page 132.*

**3** Match the actions with the pictures.

_a_ 1. You put your clothes in this.

____ 2. You find your train's departure time and track number here.

____ 3. You look for this to find your train.

____ 4. You ask questions here.

____ 5. You buy your ticket here.

____ 6. You can sit here to wait for your train.

**4** Write the words.

| | | | |
|---|---|---|---|
| departure board | suitcase | track number | waiting area |
| information desk | ticket booth | train station | |

Chandra's aunt in Chicago broke her leg. Chandra has

to go to Chicago to help her aunt. First, Chandra packs

her _____suitcase_____ . Then, she goes to the
    1.

_____ .
    2.

At the train station, Chandra goes to the _____
                                                        3.

to ask questions about trains to Chicago. Next, she goes to the

_____ to buy her ticket. Finally, she looks at the
    4.

_____ to find the time of the next train. It leaves in
    5.

one hour.

Chandra sits in the _____ and reads a book. Finally, it's time
                            6.

to go. Chandra looks for the _____ for the train to Chicago.
                                      7.

Then, she gets on the train and finds a seat. It takes four hours to get to

Chicago. Chandra will probably take a long nap!

*Check your answers. See page 132.*

# *How often? How long?*

**1** Read the questions. Look at the train schedule. Circle the answers.

**Los Angeles Unity Station**
Pacific Express – San Diego to Los Angeles

| MONDAY THROUGH FRIDAY | | |
|---|---|---|
| Departs San Diego | Arrives Los Angeles | Duration |
| 12:10 p.m. | 2:55 p.m. | 2 H 45 M |
| 3:10 p.m. | 5:55 p.m. | 2 H 45 M |
| 6:10 p.m. | 9:10 p.m. | 3 H |
| 9:10 p.m. | 1:25 a.m. | 4 H 15 M |
| SATURDAY AND SUNDAY | | |
| 6:45 a.m. | 9:45 a.m. | 3 H |
| 2:26 p.m. | 4:26 p.m. | 2 H |
| 6:10 p.m. | 9:35 p.m. | 3 H 25 M |

1. How often does the train go from San Diego to Los Angeles on the weekend?
   a. three times a day
   b. four times a day
   c. ten times a day

2. How long does it take to go from San Diego to Los Angeles on the 3:10 p.m. train?
   a. two hours and 45 minutes
   b. three hours
   c. four hours and 10 minutes

3. How often does the train go from San Diego to Los Angeles on weekdays?
   a. three times a day
   b. four times a day
   c. seven times a day

4. How long does it take to go from San Diego to Los Angeles on the 6:45 a.m. train on the weekend?
   a. two hours
   b. two hours and 25 minutes
   c. three hours

*Check your answers. See page 132.*

**2** Match the questions with the answers. Use the schedule in Exercise 1.

1. How often do trains go from San Diego to Los Angeles on weekdays? __f__

2. How long does it take to go to Los Angeles on the 9:10 p.m. train? __a__

3. How often do you take the train to Los Angeles? __b__

4. How long does it take to drive from San Diego to Los Angeles? __e__

5. How often do the trains go to Los Angeles on the weekend? __d__

6. How long does it take to go to Los Angeles on the Saturday afternoon train? __c__

a. It takes four hours and 15 minutes.

b. I take the train there once or twice a month.

c. It takes two hours.

d. They go to Los Angeles three times a day.

e. It takes a long time to drive there.

f. They go every three hours.

**3** Read the chart. Write the questions.

|  | How often? | How long? |
| --- | --- | --- |
| drive to the beach | twice a month | one hour |
| walk to the park | three or four times a week | half an hour |
| go downtown by bus | every day | 45 minutes |

1. **A** _How often do you drive to the beach?_ _____

   **B** Twice a month.

   **A** _How long does it take to drive to the beach?_ _____

   **B** It takes about one hour.

2. **A** _____

   **B** About three or four times a week.

   **A** _____

   **B** About half an hour.

3. **A** _____

   **B** Every day.

   **A** _____

   **B** About 45 minutes.

Check your answers. See page 132.

**1** Put the words in order by frequency.

| always | never | often | rarely | sometimes |

0% ←————————————————————————————————→ 100%

1. ___*never*___   2. _____   3. _____   4. _____   5. _____

**2** Read the chart. Complete the sentences. Use the words from Exercise 1.

| English 201 | September–October | Number of classes: 45 |
|---|---|---|
| **Name** | Number of times late | |
| Wang Jie | 40 | |
| Ayuko | 37 | |
| Diana | 0 | |
| Arturo | 3 | |
| Marisol | 45 | |
| Pedro | 20 | |

1. Ayuko is ___*often*___ late for class.

2. Ayuko _____ arrives on time.

3. Marisol is _____ late for class.

4. Marisol _____ arrives on time.

5. Diana is _____ on time for class.

6. Diana _____ arrives late.

7. Pedro is _____ late for class.

8. Pedro _____ arrives on time.

9. Arturo _____ arrives late.

10. Arturo is _____ on time.

11. Wang Jie is _____ late.

12. Wang Jie _____ arrives on time.

*Check your answers. See page 132.*

**3** Read the chart. Answer the questions.

| Edwin | Never | Rarely | Usually | Always |
|---|---|---|---|---|
| walks to school | | | | ✓ |
| drives to school | ✓ | | | |
| eats lunch at 1:00 p.m. | | ✓ | | |
| eats dinner at home | | | ✓ | |
| goes to sleep at 10:00 p.m. | | | ✓ | |

1. *A* How often does Edwin walk to school?

   *B* *He always walks to school.*

2. *A* How often does Edwin drive to school?

   *B* _____

3. *A* How often does Edwin eat lunch at 1:00 p.m.?

   *B* _____

4. *A* How often does Edwin eat dinner at home?

   *B* _____

5. *A* How often does Edwin go to sleep at 10:00 p.m.?

   *B* _____

**4** Read the sentences. Circle *Yes* or *No*.

1. Linda goes out to a restaurant about twice a year.
   a. Linda rarely goes out to a restaurant.    (Yes)    No
   b. Linda always eats at home.                 Yes     No

2. Fred's car is very old. It often breaks down. Fred takes the bus to work
   when his car is broken down. He drives his car to work when it is fixed.
   a. Fred never drives to work.                 Yes     No
   b. Fred often takes the bus.                  Yes     No

3. Our favorite lunch place is Sam's Sandwich Shop. We go there about
   three times a week. On the other days, we bring our lunch from home.
   a. We always eat lunch out.                   Yes     No
   b. We sometimes bring our lunch.              Yes     No

4. I take my children to the park two or three times a month.
   a. We sometimes go to the park.               Yes     No
   b. We go to the park every day.               Yes     No

Check your answers. See page 132.

**1** Read the postcard. Circle the answers.

Dear Nina,

   We're having a wonderful time in Miami. We always have lots of fun here. We usually stay with Mariam's relatives, but they're not here right now. This time we're staying at a hotel. We usually come to Miami two or three times a year. Layla always wants to go shopping at Miami International Mall. She likes to buy souvenirs there. Ali never wants to go shopping. He wants to go swimming. Mariam and I like to go sightseeing, but the children rarely go with us. I always take lots of pictures. We'll show you our pictures next week!

Love from us,

Khalid

1. Khalid and his family _____ go to Miami.
   a. never
   b. rarely
   c. often
   d. always

2. _____ always wants to go shopping.
   a. Ali
   b. Khalid
   c. Layla
   d. Mariam

3. Khalid always _____.
   a. goes shopping
   b. goes sightseeing
   c. goes swimming
   d. takes lots of pictures

4. Khalid and Mariam rarely _____.
   a. go sightseeing together
   b. go sightseeing with the children
   c. stay with Mariam's relatives
   d. take pictures

**2** Circle the answers. Use the information in Exercise 3.

1. The name of Khalid's wife is **Mariam** / **Layla**.

2. Khalid and his family are staying **with relatives** / **at a hotel**.

3. Khalid and his family **know** / **don't know** Miami very well.

4. Khalid and **Layla** / **Mariam** go sightseeing together.

Check your answers. See page 133.

**3** Complete the sentences. Use the correct form of the verbs in the box.

| buy | go | stay | take | write |

1. Lee usually ____*goes*____ swimming on Saturday afternoon.
2. Ralph sometimes _____ with relatives in San Francisco.
3. Jon always _____ pictures when he's on vacation.
4. Do you like to _____ sightseeing in a new place?
5. My son rarely wants to _____ shopping with me.
6. I often _____ souvenirs when I'm on vacation.
7. How many suitcases do you usually _____ with you?
8. Don't forget to _____ postcards to me from New York City.
9. Marco sometimes _____ at a hotel when he travels.

**4** Number the sentences in the correct order. Then write the conversation below.

_____ It usually takes about three hours by plane.
_____ Where do you usually go?
_____ I go on vacation once a year.
_____ Oh, yes! It takes two days by car.
_____ How long does it take to get there?
__1__ How often do you go on vacation?
_____ Do you always go by plane?
_____ I usually go to Denver to see my parents.

A  *How often do you go on vacation?* _____
B  _____
A  _____
B  _____
A  _____
B  _____
A  _____
B  _____

Check your answers. See page 133.

**1** Write the questions.

1. go to / Miami / How often / trains / do / ?

   *How often do trains go to Miami?*

2. does / it / San Francisco / How long / take / to get to / ?

   _____

3. to drive to / take / does / it / Detroit / How long / ?

   _____

4. go to / does / the bus / How often / Boston / ?

   _____

5. do / you / your relatives / visit / How often / in Houston / ?

   _____

6. do / stay / you / Where / usually / ?

   _____

7. usually / there / do / you / What / do / ?

   _____

**2** Write the number of the question in Exercise 1 next to the correct answer.

a. Once or twice a year. __5__        e. We always stay with my relatives. ____

b. They go every hour. ____           f. It takes about seven hours. ____

c. We often go sightseeing. ____      g. It takes about two hours by car. ____

d. It goes three times a day. ____

**3** Read the story about Liz.

## Liz's Life

Liz lives in San Antonio, Texas. Every year, Liz goes to Denver to see her mother and father. She usually stays in Denver for about a week. Liz misses her parents. She rarely has time off from work to visit them. But Liz has a very good job in San Antonio. She works as a receptionist in a printing company. She is very happy there.

*Check your answers. See page 133.*

## 4 Answer the questions about Liz.

1. How often does Liz visit her parents? *Every year.*

2. How long does she usually stay in Denver? _____

3. How often does Liz have time off from work? _____

4. How does Liz feel about her job in San Antonio? _____

## 5 Write the durations.

| Start | Stop | |
|-------|------|---|
| 12:00 | 1:05 | 1. *one hour and five minutes* |
| 8:00 | 9:45 | 2. |
| 9:00 | 9:09 | 3. |
| 4:00 | 5:07 | 4. |
| 4:30 | 5:00 | 5. |
| 6:00 | 7:12 | 6. |

## 6 Complete the story.

Martin usually __*goes*__ to work by train.
     1. go

It _____ about 30 minutes to get to
    2. take

work by train. Martin _____ his house
              3. leave

at 7:15 a.m. He usually _____ to work
           4. get

at 8:00. He _____ to be late for work.
     5. not like

Sometimes the trains _____ late. Martin
         6. be

_____ his laptop computer on the train.
 7. use

He rarely _____ on the train in the
     8. sleep

morning. Sometimes he _____ a nap on
         9. take

the trip home. He never _____ to people
        10. talk

on the train. Martin _____ the train. He
       11. like

_____ to drive to work.
  12. not like

Check your answers. See page 133.

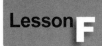

**1** Read the chart. Write the questions and answers.

### How Students Get to School Each Morning

| Name | Transportation | Why | Duration | Arrival at school |
|------|----------------|-----|----------|-------------------|
| Mai | | • Goes every half hour<br>• Cheap | • 10 minutes to bus stop<br>• 10 minutes on bus | • Usually 10 minutes early<br>• Sometimes late |
| Shen Hui | | • No waiting<br>• Good exercise | • 20 minutes | • Always on time |
| Phillipe | | • No waiting<br>• Good exercise | • 35 minutes | • Always on time |
| Sara | | • Goes every 5 minutes<br>• Usually on time | • 15 minutes to subway<br>• 7 minutes on subway | • Rarely late |
| Zoraida | | • No waiting | • 7 minutes in car<br>• 2–15 minutes to park car | • Often 5 minutes late |

1. How often / bus / go  *How often does the bus go?*  _____
   *It goes every half hour.*  _____

2. How / Shen Hui / get to school  _____
   _____

3. How long / to get / from Shen Hui's house / to school / by bicycle  _____
   _____

4. How often / Phillipe / arrive on time  _____
   _____

5. How long / to get / from Sara's house / to school / by subway  _____
   _____

6. How / Zoraida / get to school  _____
   _____

*Check your answers. See page 133.*

**2** Read the paragraphs. Find the person. Use the chart in Exercise 1.

1.
I get good exercise every day. I'm always on time. It takes 20 minutes to get to class every day.

Who am I? _Shen Hui_

2.
I don't like to wait for buses or subways. I go to school with my friends. It takes only seven minutes to get to school from my home. I'm often late for class because we can't find a parking space.

Who am I? _____

3.
I don't like to wait for buses or subways. I like to be on time. I also like to get up early. It takes over half an hour to get to class from my home, but I am never late.

Who am I? _____

4.
It only takes 20 minutes to get to class from my apartment. Sometimes I'm late because my transportation is late. But it is cheap!

Who am I? _____

5.
I'm rarely late because my transportation goes every five minutes. If I miss one, there's another one in five minutes.

Who am I? _____

**3** Write the words. Use each word only once. Use the chart in Exercise 1.

| always | never | often | rarely | sometimes | usually |
|--------|-------|-------|--------|-----------|---------|

1. Sara is ___usually___ on time.

2. Shen Hui is _____ on time.

3. The subway is _____ late.

4. The bus is _____ late.

5. Zoraida is _____ five minutes late.

6. Phillipe is _____ late.

Check your answers. See page 133.

## Lesson A *Get ready*

**1** Complete the words

1. cl <u>*a*</u> ss p <u>*i*</u> ct <u>*u*</u> r <u>*e*</u>
2. f ___ m ___ l ___
3. g r ___ d ___ ___ t ___ ___ n
4. b ___ b ___
5. p h ___ t ___ ___ l b ___ m
6. w ___ d d ___ n g

**2** Look at the pictures. Write the words from Exercise 1.

1. Our children's ___*photo album*___

2. Jim and Justin at their high school _____ – 6/5/99

3. Our _____ – 11/89

4. Jim and Deb's _____ day – 5/9/05

5. Jim and Justin's _____ – June '87

6. Jim and Deb's _____ boy, Carl! 12/11/09

*Check your answers. See page 133.*

**3** Look at the pictures in Exercise 2. Circle the answers.

1. Jim and Justin became friends ____ .
   a. in school *(circled)*
   b. in the hospital
   c. at work

2. They graduated from high school on ____ .
   a. May 5, 1999
   b. May 6, 1999
   c. June 5, 1999

3. Jim and Deb got married in ____ .
   a. 1995
   b. 2005
   c. 2007

4. Jim and Deb had a baby on ____ .
   a. December 7, 2001
   b. November 12, 2009
   c. December 11, 2009

5. Jim has ____ .
   a. no brothers or sisters
   b. one sister
   c. one sister and one brother

**4** Complete the sentences.

| albums | baby | class | family | graduation | pictures | wedding |
|--------|------|-------|--------|------------|----------|---------|

**A** Are these your photo ____*albums*____ ?
1.
You have a lot of them.

**B** Yes, we took a lot of _____ .
2.
Let's look at this one. It's about Jim and Lily.

**A** Are these their _____ pictures?
3.
They were beautiful babies!

**B** Thank you. Oh, here's Jim's 4th grade _____ picture.
4.
That's his best friend, Justin, next to him.

**A** And here they are again! Is this Jim's high school _____ ?
5.

**B** Yes, it is.

**A** Why don't these pages have any pictures?

**B** We're going to put Lily's _____ pictures there someday.
6.

**A** Oh, that's nice. What a wonderful _____ ! You're lucky!
7.

Check your answers. See page 133.

## Lesson B | When did you move here?

*Study the chart on page 124.*

**1** Write the verbs in the past tense.

1. move _____moved_____    6. start _____

2. have _____    7. get _____

3. begin _____    8. leave _____

4. study _____    9. meet _____

5. find _____    10. graduate _____

**2** Complete the chart. Use the past tense forms from Exercise 1.

| Regular verbs (-*ed* verbs) | Irregular verbs (not -*ed* verbs) |
|---|---|
| moved | had |
|  |  |
|  |  |
|  |  |
|  |  |
|  |  |

**3** Answer the questions. Use the words in parentheses.

1. When did you move here?

   (in 2000) _I moved here in 2000._

2. When did Ken start college?

   (in September) _____

3. When did you and your husband meet?

   (in 1988) _____

4. When did you get married?

   (in 1990) _____

5. When did your children begin taking English classes?

   (last year) _____

6. When did Norma leave for vacation?

   (on Saturday) _____

*Check your answers. See page 133.*

**4** Read Elsa's time line. Write the questions or the answers.

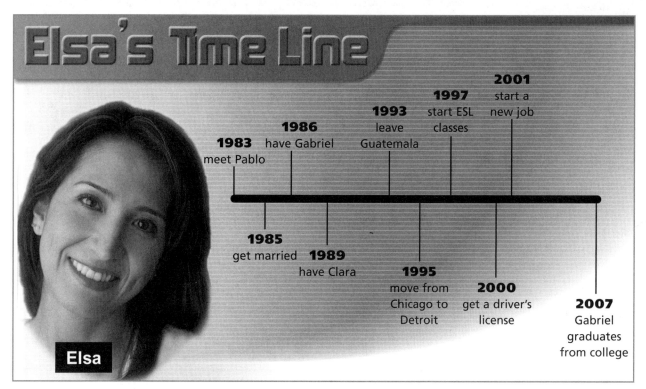

## Elsa's Time Line

Elsa

- **1983** meet Pablo
- **1985** get married
- **1986** have Gabriel
- **1989** have Clara
- **1993** leave Guatemala
- **1995** move from Chicago to Detroit
- **1997** start ESL classes
- **2000** get a driver's license
- **2001** start a new job
- **2007** Gabriel graduates from college

1. **A** *When did Elsa meet Pablo?*

   **B** Elsa met Pablo in 1983.

2. **A** _____

   **B** They got married in 1985.

3. **A** When did they have Gabriel?

   **B** _____

4. **A** _____

   **B** They had Clara in 1989.

5. **A** When did they leave Guatemala?

   **B** _____

6. **A** When did they move from Chicago to Detroit?

   **B** _____

7. **A** _____

   **B** Elsa started taking ESL classes in 1997.

8. **A** When did Elsa get her driver's license?

   **B** _____

Check your answers. See page 134.

# Lesson C  *He graduated two years ago.*

**1** Complete the chart for events in the past.

| four days | night | a month | April 11th, 1960 | Saturday |
|-----------|-------|---------|------------------|----------|
| March 23rd | a week | July | the afternoon | the morning |
| 6:15 | 1999 | May 9th | six months | half past four |
| December | two years | Wednesday | noon | |

| ago | in | on | at |
|-----|-----|-----|-----|
| *four days* | *December* | *March 23rd* | *6:15* |
| | | | |
| | | | |
| | | | |
| | | | |

**2** Circle the answers.

1. Jeff and Marlena got married **ago** / **last** Saturday.

2. Their wedding was **in** / **on** February 1st.

3. The wedding was **at** / **this** noon.

4. They started planning the wedding eight months **ago** / **last**.

5. Marlena found her dress **in** / **on** December.

6. They left for their honeymoon **on** / **this** morning.

7. They need to return **before** / **on** Jeff's new job begins.

8. His new job begins **in** / **on** Monday, February 10th.

9. He quit his old job just **before** / **last** they got married.

10. Marlena started her job three months **after** / **ago**.

Check your answers. See page 134.

**3** Read Walter's calendar. Today is May 23rd. Complete the sentences. Use *in*, *on*, *at*, *ago*, *last*, *before*, or *after*.

| | | | May | | | |
|---|---|---|---|---|---|---|
| **Sunday** | **Monday** | **Tuesday** | **Wednesday** | **Thursday** | **Friday** | **Saturday** |
| **10** shop for my sister's graduation present | **11** begin new job - 8:00 a.m. | **12** fix my car after work | **13** study for citizenship exam | **14** take citizenship exam - 1:15 | **15** basketball game - 7:30 p.m. | **16** Carina's graduation - 2:00 dinner with family - 6:30 |
| **17** | **18** | **19** take driving test for license - 8:00 a.m. | **20** doctor's appointment - 4:30 | **21** take books back to library | **22** lunch with Carina and her boyfriend | **23** lunch with Mario - noon |

1. Walter had dinner with his sister Carina and her boyfriend _____*last*_____ night.

2. He took his citizenship exam _____ Thursday, May 14th.

3. The test started _____ 1:15.

4. Walter fixed his car two days ___*before*___ he took the citizenship exam.

5. He fixed the car ___*in*___ the evening.

6. Carina's graduation was a week ___*ago*___ .

7. The family had dinner together ___*after*___ Carina's graduation.

8. Walter began his new job ___*last*___ week.

**4** Answer the questions. Use the words in parentheses and the calendar in Exercise 3.

1. When did Walter take his driving test?

(ago) _He took his driving test four days ago._

2. When did Walter shop for his sister's graduation present?

(last week) _____

3. When did Walter play basketball?

(Friday, May 15th) _____

4. When did Walter have a doctor's appointment?

(4:30) _____

5. When did Walter take his books back to the library?

(ago) _____

Check your answers. See page 134.

# Lesson D Reading

**1** Read the story. Write the correct past tense form of the verb.

> ## P.C.
>
> Alma ___immigrated___ to the U.S. ten years ago. In Chile, Alma
> 1. immigrate
>
> _____ with computers. Alma _____ English
> 2. work                                          3. start
>
> classes after she came to the U.S. Alma _____ English for
> 4. study
>
> three years. Then, Alma _____ computer classes. Alma
> 5. begin
>
> _____ a wonderful man named Elmer in her computer class.
> 6. meet
>
> Alma and Elmer _____ in love. After three months, they
> 7. fall
>
> _____ engaged. They _____ married three years
> 8. get                                    9. get
>
> ago. After they got married, they _____ good jobs in a small
> 10. find
>
> computer company. One year later, they got promoted. After two years,
>
> they _____ a small computer business called PC Home
> 11. start
>
> Repairs. Last night, Alma and Elmer _____ a baby girl.
> 12. have
>
> They _____ to name their baby Patricia Catherina. They
> 13. decide
>
> will call her P.C. for short!

**2** Answer the questions. Use the information from Exercise 1.

1. When did Alma immigrate to the U.S.?

   _She immigrated ten years ago._

2. When did Alma start English classes?

   _____

3. How long did Alma study English?

   _____

4. When did Alma and Elmer get married?

   _____

5. When did Alma and Elmer find jobs?

   _____

Check your answers. See page 134.

68 Unit 6

**3** Number the pictures of Alma's life in the correct order. Use the information from Exercise 1.

a. _____

b. _____

c. _____

d. _1_

e. _____

f. _____

**4** Complete the sentences. Use the information from Exercise 1.

| | | |
|---|---|---|
| fell in love | got married | immigrated |
| get a divorce | got promoted | retire |
| got engaged | had a baby | started a business |

1. Ten years ago, Alma _____immigrated_____ to the U.S.

2. Alma and Elmer met in their computer class. Then they _Fell in Love_.

3. Three years ago, Alma and Elmer _got a married_.

4. Before they got married, Alma and Elmer _got engaged_.

5. One year after they got jobs, Alma and Elmer _get a promote_.

6. Two years after they got jobs, Alma and Elmer quit and _starte a business_.

7. Last night, Alma and Elmer _Had a baby_.

8. When Alma and Elmer are 65, they will probably _retire_.

9. They hope they will never _get a divorced_.

Check your answers. See page 134.

# Lesson **E** *Writing*

**1** Complete the paragraph. Use the simple past.

| After | have | in | learn | open | take |
|-------|------|-----|-------|------|------|
| find | In | last | on | start | work |

## A Dream Comes True

Hisun Shen immigrated from China to the U.S. _____*on*_____ January
1.

5, 1998. She _____ a lot of plans. She _____ English classes
2. 3.

_____ February 1998. She _____ English classes for two
4. 5.

years. She also _____ as a waitress in a Chinese restaurant.
6.

_____ September 1999, she began vocational school. She
7.

_____ to be a chef in a Chinese restaurant. _____ two years,
8. 9.

she graduated from that program. Then, she _____ a job as a chef
10.

in a Chinese restaurant. That was in September 2001. She worked there

for six years. But Hisun had a dream. Finally, _____ week, Hisun
11.

_____ her own restaurant. She calls her restaurant Hisun's Dream.
12.

**2** Complete the time line for Hisun.

| | |
|---|---|
| a. began vocational school | d. started English classes |
| b. came to the U.S. | e. worked as a chef |
| c. graduated from vocational school | f. worked as a waitress |

**Hisun's time line**

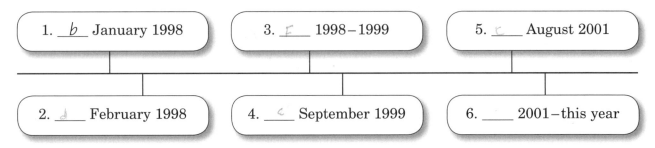

1. _*b*_ January 1998       3. _*f*_ 1998–1999       5. _*c*_ August 2001

2. _*d*_ February 1998       4. _*c*_ September 1999       6. _____ 2001–this year

*Check your answers. See page 134.*

**3** Answer the questions. Use the information from Exercises 1 and 2.
Write your answers in two different ways.

1. When did Hisun leave China?

   *On January 5, 1998, she left China.*

   *She left China on January 5, 1998.*

2. When did she begin English classes?

   _____

   _____

3. How long did she take English classes?

   _____

   _____

4. When did she begin vocational school?

   _____

   _____

5. In what year did she graduate from vocational school?

   _____

   _____

6. When did she find a job as a chef?

   _____

   _____

7. When did she open her own restaurant?

   _____

   _____

Check your answers. See page 134.

# *Another view*

**1** Read the questions. Look at the school application. Circle the answers.

## LCC

### LAGUNA COMMUNITY COLLEGE

First name ___Lin Tao___ Middle initial ___B___ Last name ___Ho___

Birthdate (Mo/Day/Yr) ___9/23/84___ Male ___X___ Female _____

Street address or P.O. box ___616 Capstone Street___

City ___Laguna___ State ___Washington___ Zip code ___98103___

E-mail address ___compwiz@cup.org___ Telephone ___206-555-1151___

Semester ___Fall 2008___

Course of study ___Computer Technology___

Educational goal ___2-year certificate___

Entry level ___First-time student in college___

High school education ___GED completed 6/12/07___

Is your primary language English? Yes (No)

If you circled "No": Primary language ___Mandarin___

What level is your English?

Beginner     Low-intermediate     Intermediate     High-intermediate     (Advanced)

Date of application: ___5/23/08___

---

1. When was Lin Tao born?
   a. 9/3/80
   (b.) 9/23/84
   c. 6/12/07
   d. 5/23/08

2. What does Lin Tao want to study?
   a. computer technology
   b. Mandarin
   c. English
   d. GED

3. When did Lin Tao get his GED?
   a. on June 6, 2007
   b. on June 12, 2007
   c. on December 6, 2007
   d. on May 23, 2008

4. How long is this course of study?
   a. two years
   b. two semesters
   c. two classes
   d. two weeks

5. What semester is this application for?
   a. spring
   b. summer
   c. fall
   d. winter

6. What level is Lin Tao's English?
   a. beginner
   b. intermediate
   c. high-intermediate
   d. advanced

*Check your answers. See page 134.*

## 2 Match the parts of the idioms.

1. They had stars _a_      a. in their eyes.

2. He popped ____      b. feet before the wedding.

3. She got cold ____      c. sailing.

4. They tied ____      d. the rocks.

5. For a while, their marriage was on ____      e. the knot last month.

6. Most of the time, it was smooth ____      f. the question.

## 3 Complete the story. Use the idioms from Exercise 2.

### Love on the Rocks

Gretchen and Kevin had **1.** love. They **4.** one week when they first met. They fell in love later. It was for a while. very quickly. Kevin **2.** after But after six months, their marriage only one week. At first, Gretchen and was **6.** . Soon, they got a Kevin were very happy. But then, divorce. Now Kevin and Gretchen they both got **3.** . They stopped say, "Always wait longer than a dating for one year. After one year, week to change your life!" they met again. They were still in

1. _stars in their eyes_ _____

2. _____

3. _____

4. _____

5. _____

6. _____

Check your answers. See page 134.

**Time  73**

# Get ready

**Shopping**

## 1 Complete the words.

1. s t __o__ v __e__
2. s ___ l ___ s p ___ r s ___ n
3. s ___ f ___
4. p ___ ___ n ___
5. c ___ s t ___ m ___ r
6. ___ p p l ___ ___ n c ___ ___
7. f ___ r n ___ t ___ r ___
8. p r ___ c ___ t ___ g

## 2 Look at the pictures. Write the words from Exercise 1.

_____ sofa _____    _____

_____  _____  _____  _____

_____    _____

**Check your answers. See page 135.**

**3** Complete the conversation. Use the words from Exercises 1 and 2.

**A** Good afternoon. My name is Milton and I'm a _____salesperson_____ .
1.

Are you a new _____ ?
2.

**B** Yes, I am. I'm looking for some _____ .
3.

**A** This is the right place to shop! We have great furniture and _____ .
4.

**B** Well, I'm looking for a green _____ for my living room. A used one.
5.

**A** We have some in the next room. Is there anything else you need?

**B** Well, maybe a secondhand _____ for my children to play.
6.

**A** Look over there. And how about a new _____ for your kitchen?
7.

This one's on sale right now. It's 30% off!

**B** But how much is it? Where's the _____ ? I can't spend
8.

very much money.

**A** No problem. Our prices are the cheapest in town! Right this way. . . .

**4** Look at the bold word. Cross out the word that is different.

| **Appliances** | stove | refrigerator | dishwasher | ~~piano~~ |
| --- | --- | --- | --- | --- |
| **Furniture** | chair | car | sofa | table |
| **People** | customer | salesperson | price tag | cashier |

Check your answers. See page 135.

## Lesson B — *The brown sofa is bigger.*

*Study the chart on page 127.*

**1** Complete the conversations.

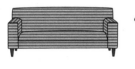

1. **A** The striped sofa is big.

   **B** But the black sofa is _____*bigger*_____ .

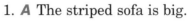
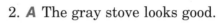

2. **A** The gray stove looks good.

   **B** But the white stove looks _____ .

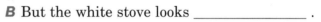

3. **A** The white refrigerator is heavy.

   **B** But the gray refrigerator is _____ .

4. **A** The plaid chair is comfortable.

   **B** But the checked chair is _____ .

**2** Complete the conversation. Use comparatives.

**A** Which chair is ___*more comfortable*___ ? The blue chair or the red chair?
   <sub>1. comfortable</sub>

**B** I don't know. But the blue chair is _____ .
   <sub>2. pretty</sub>

   I like the pattern and the color.

**A** I do, too. Is it _____ ?
   <sub>3. expensive</sub>

**B** Don't worry about the price. This is a thrift shop! Everything is

   _____ than in a department store.
   <sub>4. cheap</sub>

**A** Right! Well, the red chair is _____ than the blue chair.
   <sub>5. big</sub>

   It's _____ , too.
   <sub>6. heavy</sub>

**B** I want the blue chair.

**A** OK. Let's ask about the price.

*Check your answers. See page 135.*

**3** Answer the questions.

# MOVING SOON!
## BUY MY FURNITURE!
### 55 LINCOLN AVE.

**TABLES!**
- A kitchen table for 4 people
- A dining room table for 8 people

**CHAIRS!**
- Red chairs for children
- White chairs for the kitchen

**APPLIANCES!**
- Stove: $200
- Refrigerator: $250

**SOFAS!**
- A green sofa for 6 people
- A white sofa for 3 people

**DESKS!**
- A blue desk – 1982
- A silver desk – 2005

**LAMPS!**
- A green floor lamp
- A black table lamp

1. **A** Which table is bigger?

   **B** *The dining room table is bigger.*

2. **A** Which chairs are smaller?

   **B** _____

3. **A** Which appliance is more expensive?

   **B** _____

4. **A** Which desk is older?

   **B** _____

5. **A** Which sofa is longer?

   **B** _____

6. **A** Which lamp is shorter?

   **B** _____

*Check your answers. See page 135.*

# *The yellow chair is the cheapest.*

*Study the chart on page 127.*

**1** Complete the chart. Write the comparative and superlative forms of the adjectives.

| | Adjective | Comparative | Superlative |
|---|---|---|---|
| 1. | expensive | *more expensive* | *the most expensive* |
| 2. | cheap | | |
| 3. | friendly | | |
| 4. | good | | |
| 5. | new | | |
| 6. | heavy | | |
| 7. | low | | |
| 8. | beautiful | | |
| 9. | pretty | | |
| 10. | crowded | | |
| 11. | comfortable | | |
| 12. | nice | | |

**2** Complete the conversations. Use superlatives.

1. Furniture First has _____the lowest_____ prices of all the furniture stores.
   (low)

2. Robinson's Furniture has _____ chairs.
   (comfortable)

3. Jay Mart's clothes are _____ clothes in the mall.
   (good)

4. Curto's has _____ appliances in town.
   (expensive)

5. Which store has _____ salespeople?
   (nice)

6. Bella's clothes are _____ in the mall.
   (pretty)

7. The furniture at Secondhand Row is _____ in town.
   (cheap)

8. Jilly's Jeans is _____ clothing store here.
   (small)

9. Appliance World is _____ of all the appliance stores.
   (crowded)

10. The SuperPlus TVs are _____ TVs in the store.
    (heavy)

*Check your answers. See page 135.*

**3** Complete the chart.

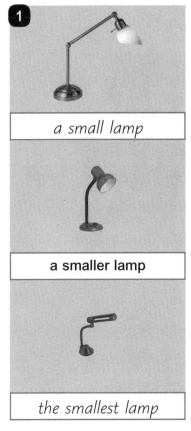

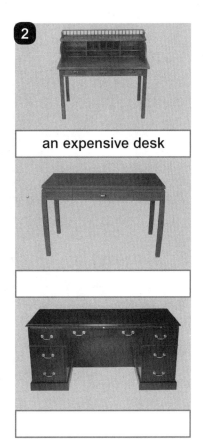

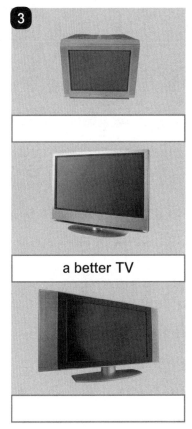

| | | |
|---|---|---|
| *a small lamp* | **an expensive desk** | |
| **a smaller lamp** | | **a better TV** |
| *the smallest lamp* | | |

**4** Answer the questions.

## Clothing for Today's Woman

A. jeans skirt $40　　B. tennis skirt $55　　C. evening skirt $150

1. Which skirt is the most expensive?

   *The evening skirt is the most expensive.*

2. Which skirt is the longest?

   _____

3. Which skirt is the cheapest?

   _____

4. Which skirt is the shortest?

   _____

Check your answers. See page 135.

**1** Read the newspaper article. Complete the sentences.

# Centerville's Newest Old Store

by Joe Jordan

Antique Alley is the _____*newest*_____ store in Centerville. Antique Alley
             1. new

opened on May 1st, and now it's having a _____ sale. Everything
                      2. big

is 50% to 75% off. Those are the _____ prices for old furniture in Centerville.
                3. good

I visited Antique Alley yesterday. The furniture is _____ . For me, the
                    4. beautiful

_____ thing in the store was a large mirror. I didn't buy it because it was also the
  5. nice

_____ thing in the store. It was $1,300! Of course, it was also the _____
  6. expensive                              7. old

thing in the store. It was 300 years old. But there were lots of things that were _____
                                        8. cheap

than the mirror. The _____ thing was a _____ lamp for only $12.95.
         9. cheap                10. small

Visit Antique Alley this weekend. You'll be surprised at what you find.

**2** Answer the questions.

1. What is the name of the store?

   *The name of the store is Antique Alley.*

2. When did it open?

   _____

3. What was the most expensive thing in the store?

   _____

4. How much was it?

   _____

5. What was the cheapest thing in the store?

   _____

6. How much was it?

   _____

Check your answers. See page 135.

# 3 Complete the puzzle.

| | | |
|---|---|---|
| bookcase | entertainment center | recliner |
| china cabinet | furniture | sofa bed |
| dresser | mirror | table |

## Down

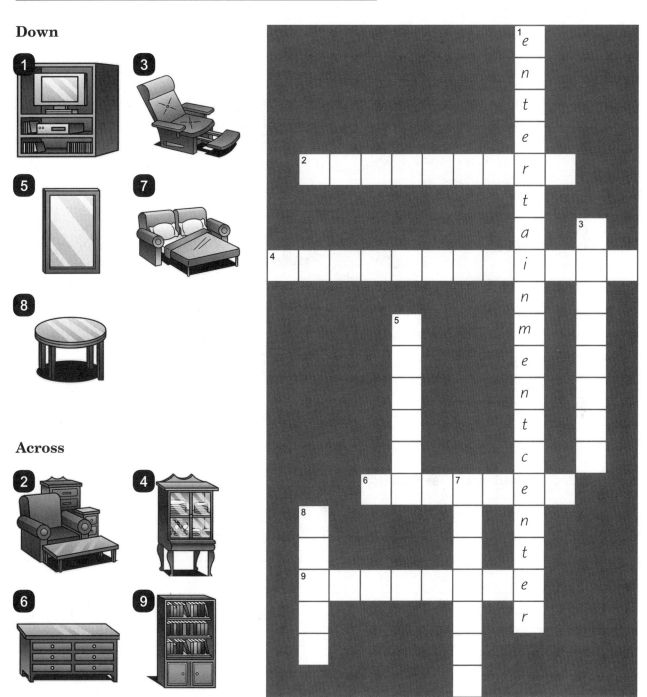

## Across

Check your answers. See page 135.

**1** Read the note. Look at the picture. Answer the questions.

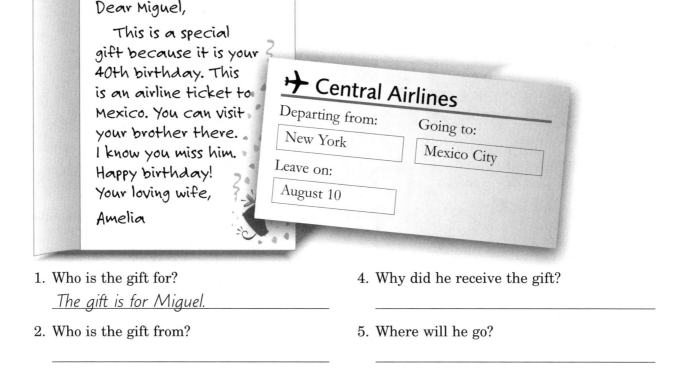

Dear Miguel,

This is a special gift because it is your 40th birthday. This is an airline ticket to Mexico. You can visit your brother there. I know you miss him. Happy birthday! Your loving wife,

Amelia

✈ **Central Airlines**

Departing from:

New York

Going to:

Mexico City

Leave on:

August 10

1. Who is the gift for?
   _The gift is for Miguel._

2. Who is the gift from?

3. What did she give him?

4. Why did he receive the gift?

5. Where will he go?

6. What day will he leave?

**2** Combine the sentences. Use *because*.

1. I bought the red sofa. It was the most comfortable.
   _I bought the red sofa because it was the most comfortable._

2. Sandra gave her sister a pair of earrings. It was her birthday.

3. Mr. and Mrs. Chung shop at the Clothes Corner. It's the nicest store.

4. Roberto bought the brown recliner. It was on sale.

5. I bought an entertainment center. It was 50% off.

*Check your answers. See page 135.*

**3** Read the chart. Complete the sentences. Use the comparative or superlative.

| CENTERVILLE DEPARTMENT STORES | Opened | Size | Prices | Comments |
|---|---|---|---|---|
| **Best Discounts** | 1973 | 40,000 square feet | very low | nice salespeople |
| **Smart Department Store** | 2007 | 60,000 square feet | very high | beautiful, not crowded |
| **Super Discounts** | 1952 | 20,000 square feet | medium | crowded |

Yesterday, I needed to buy a lot of things, so I went shopping at Best Discounts. Smart Department Store is _____*bigger*_____ than Best Discounts,
1. big
but the salespeople are _____ at Best Discounts. Also, the
2. nice
prices at Best Discounts are _____ than at Smart Department
3. good
Store. Smart Department Store is _____ than Best Discounts,
4. new
and it's also _____ than Best Discounts, but the prices are
5. beautiful
_____ .
6. high

I never go to Super Discounts. It's the _____ department store
7. old
in town. It's the _____ , and it's always the _____ .
8. small                                                9. crowded

**4** Complete the sentences. Use the chart in Exercise 3. Use the superlative.

1. (small) _____*Super Discounts*_____ is _____*the smallest*_____ .

2. (old) _____ is _____ .

3. (big) _____ is _____ .

4. (expensive) _____ is _____ .

5. (cheap) _____ is _____ .

6. (crowded) _____ is _____ .

Check your answers. See page 135.

# Lesson F  Another view

**1** Read the questions. Look at the ad. Circle the answers.

**Nick's Nearly New**

Closing Sale. 25–50% off
everything in the store.
Come and look!
Used furniture in good condition!
Hours: 9 a.m. to midnight,
7 days a week.
*Deliveries on weekends only.*

**BIG BILL'S BEST FURNITURE**

**FATHER'S DAY SALE!**

All recliners and chairs on sale.
New and used! Only the best.
30 – 40% discounts.
**FREE DELIVERY.**

Hours:
8:00 a.m. – 6:00 p.m.
Mon. – Sat.

## MODERN FURNITURE

Everything on sale! 50–80% off. China Cabinets, Bookcases, Beds,
Sofa Beds, Coffee Tables, Entertainment Centers, Kitchen Appliances.
We have it all. It's all new!

HOURS: 11:00–9:00 MONDAY THROUGH FRIDAY AND 12:00–9:00 ON SATURDAY.
BRING A VAN AND TAKE IT HOME. EXTRA FOR DELIVERY.

1. Which store has only used furniture?
   a. Big Bill's
   b. Modern Furniture
   c. Nick's Nearly New
   d. all of the above

2. Which store makes deliveries?
   a. Big Bill's
   b. Modern Furniture
   c. Nick's Nearly New
   d. all of the above

3. Which store has new and used furniture?
   a. Big Bill's
   b. Modern Furniture
   c. Nick's Nearly New
   d. all of the above

4. Which store has a Father's Day Sale?
   a. Big Bill's
   b. Modern Furniture
   c. Nick's Nearly New
   d. all of the above

5. Which store is open on Sunday?
   a. Big Bill's
   b. Modern Furniture
   c. Nick's Nearly New
   d. all of the above

6. At which store do you pay extra for delivery?
   a. Big Bill's
   b. Modern Furniture
   c. Nick's Nearly New
   d. all of the above

*Check your answers. See page 136.*

**2** Answer the questions. Use the information from Exercise 1.

1. Where can you get 50–80% off?

   *You can get 50–80% off at Modern Furniture.*

2. Where can you shop at 8:30 a.m.?

   _____

3. Which store has free delivery?

   _____

4. Which store sells only new furniture?

   _____

5. Which store is open seven days a week?

   _____

**3** Find the words.

| beautiful | comfortable | expensive | good | short |
|-----------|-------------|-----------|------|-------|
| cheap | crowded | friendly | heavy | tall |

| | | | | | | | | | | |
|---|---|---|---|---|---|---|---|---|---|---|
| g | o | o | d | o | v | e | g | h | r | l | w |
| f | s | o | e | d | a | t | b | l | r | r | s |
| c | h | v | w | f | r | i | e | n | d | l | y |
| c | o | m | f | o | r | t | a | b | l | e | o |
| h | r | t | r | d | h | a | u | l | t | x | r |
| e | t | l | d | t | l | l | t | p | r | p | c |
| a | v | o | h | c | t | l | i | o | m | e | s |
| p | d | o | u | u | a | w | f | d | e | n | i |
| f | y | e | x | o | e | a | u | f | d | s | v |
| v | o | l | c | e | e | f | l | t | f | i | r |
| e | a | i | t | f | o | a | h | e | a | v | y |
| d | l | e | v | a | c | r | o | w | d | e | d |

Check your answers. See page 136.

**1** Unscramble the letters. Write the words.

1. bla      _____*lab*_____
2. derlyor      _____
3. oc-rkerwos      _____
4. kerwal      _____

5. inensl      _____
6. tentiap      _____
7. liessupp      _____
8. hailwhreec      _____

**2** Look at the picture. Write the words from Exercise 1.

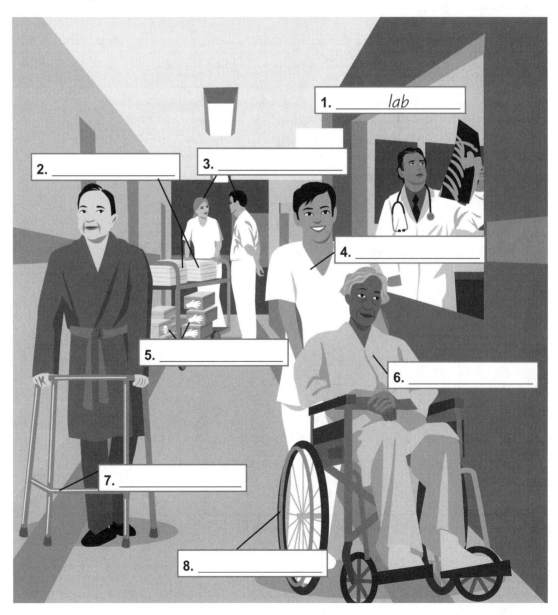

1. _____*lab*_____
2. _____
3. _____
4. _____
5. _____
6. _____
7. _____
8. _____

*Check your answers. See page 136.*

**3** Complete the sentences.

| co-workers | linens | orderly | patient | walker | wheelchair |
|---|---|---|---|---|---|

1. The ___patient___ came to the hospital with a broken leg.

2. Suzanne and her two _____ worked the night shift together.

3. Suzanne put clean _____ on the bed.

4. Because he broke his leg, Sam had to ride in a _____ .

5. The _____ took the X-rays to the lab.

6. Anne is very old. She needs to use a _____ when she walks.

**4** Look at the pictures. Complete the paragraph. Then number the pictures in the correct order.

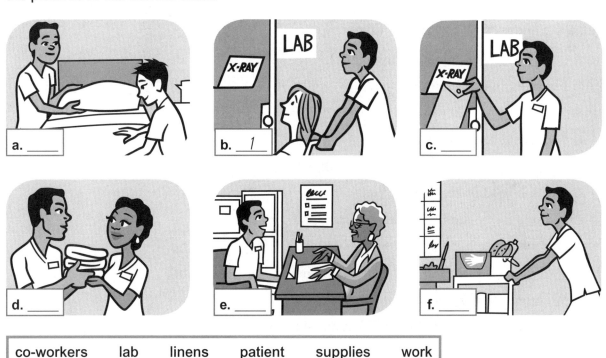

a. _____   b. _1_   c. _____

d. _____   e. _____   f. _____

| co-workers | lab | linens | patient | supplies | work |
|---|---|---|---|---|---|

Jorge had a busy afternoon at the hospital. First, he took a ___patient___
                                                          1.
to the lab. Then, he delivered boxes of _____ to the nurses. Next, he
                                              2.
picked up clean _____ for the third floor. After that, he prepared the
                    3.
rooms with David. Jorge and David are _____ . Then, Jorge picked
                                           4.
up X-rays from the _____ . Finally, he had a meeting in Human Resources.
                        5.
Jorge wants to _____ more hours.
                   6.

*Check your answers. See page 136.*

# *Where did you go last night?*

*Study the chart on page 124.*

**1** Match the questions with the answers.

1. Where did you go last night? __*c*__      a. They worked in restaurants.

2. What did you take to the party? ____      b. She cleaned the house.

3. What did Cristal do after breakfast? ____      c. I went to the movies.

4. Where did your parents meet? ____      d. He picked up a uniform.

5. What did they do after they came to the U.S.? ____      e. I took a cake to the party.

6. What did Jon pick up at your house? ____      f. We went to the beach.

7. Where did you and Andy go this morning? ____      g. They met at school.

**2** Read the answers. Write *What* or *Where*.

1. **A** ____*What*____ did you do last night?

   **B** I worked the night shift.

2. **A** _____ did you go after work?

   **B** I went out for breakfast.

3. **A** _____ did Max do after breakfast?

   **B** He took the bus to school.

4. **A** _____ did Sheila do at work this morning?

   **B** She made the beds with new linens.

5. **A** _____ did you and your family eat dinner last night?

   **B** We ate dinner at Tony's Pizzeria.

6. **A** _____ did Sheila and Max do last weekend?

   **B** They went to the park for a picnic.

*Check your answers. See page 136.*

**3** Complete the questions and answers. Use *What* or *Where* and the simple past.

**Mai**

- meet new patients in reception area – 9:00
- take the patient in Room 304 to the lab – 9:30
- make the bed in Room 304
- take patients from lab to their rooms – 10:00
- help nurses on the fourth floor – 10:45
- lunch in the cafeteria – 12:30

**Jorge**

- meet new patients in reception area – 9:00
- pick up X-rays from lab – 9:30
- deliver X-rays to doctors
- help patient in Room 310 – 10:00
- prepare rooms on the second floor – 11:30
- lunch in the cafeteria – 12:30

1. **A** _____*What*_____ did Mai and Jorge do at 9:00?

   **B** *They met new patients in the reception area.* _____

2. **A** _____ did Mai take her patient at 9:30?

   **B** _____

3. **A** _____ did Jorge do at 9:30?

   **B** _____

4. **A** _____ did Mai and Jorge do after 9:30?

   **B** Mai _____ and Jorge _____

5. **A** _____ did Jorge go at 10:00?

   **B** _____

6. **A** _____ did Jorge do in Room 310?

   **B** _____

7. **A** _____ did Mai do at 10:00?

   **B** _____

8. **A** _____ did Mai go after that?

   **B** _____

9. **A** _____ did Jorge do at 11:30?

   **B** _____

10. **A** _____ did Mai and Jorge go at 12:30?

    **B** _____

*Check your answers. See page 136.*

**1** Complete the sentences. Use *and*, *or*, or *but*.

1. Mateo has two jobs. He works in a restaurant ___*and*___ in an office.

2. We can have lunch at Sub's _____ at Carl's.

3. Gu Jan talked to his mother about his job plans, _____ he didn't talk to his father.

4. After work, Lourdes had cake _____ ice cream.

5. Mandy and Paco went to New York, _____ they didn't go to see the Statue of Liberty.

6. Ivan works the day shift _____ the night shift. He never works both shifts.

7. Sally works at the hospital during the week _____ at Pizza Mizza on the weekend.

8. At work, Ang answers the phones _____ takes messages.

**2** Combine the sentences. Use *and*, *or*, or *but*.

1. Sometimes Jun eats lunch at noon. Sometimes Jun eats lunch at 1:00.
   *Jun eats lunch at noon or at 1:00.*

2. Javier helps the nurses. He also helps the doctors.
   _____

3. Tien picks up the supplies at the warehouse. She doesn't deliver the supplies.
   _____

4. Rieko met her new co-workers this morning. She didn't meet any patients.
   _____

5. At the restaurant, Mustafa made the soup. He also made the salad.
   _____

6. Sometimes Anatoly drinks coffee. Sometimes he drinks tea.
   _____

**Check your answers. See page 136.**

**3** Read the chart. Write sentences. Use *and* or *but*, and the simple past.

| Office Assistant Duties – Friday 11/29 | | |
|---|---|---|
| Rachel | Dora | Adam |
| Prepare the meeting room<br>Pick up supplies<br>Deliver the mail | Make the coffee<br>Go to the meeting<br>Answer calls<br>Take messages | Check the office e-mail<br>Go to the meeting<br>Take notes<br>Make copies |

1. Dora / go to the meeting / take notes

   *Dora went to the meeting, but she didn't take notes.*

2. Adam / check the office e-mail / go to the meeting

   _____

3. Rachel / prepare the meeting room / make the coffee

   _____

4. Dora and Adam / go to the meeting / prepare the meeting room

   _____

5. Adam / take notes / make copies

   _____

6. Rachel / pick up supplies / deliver the mail

   _____

**4** Complete the sentences with *and*, *or*, or *but*.

| Please eat lunch at your desk and answer calls on these days: | | | | | |
|---|---|---|---|---|---|
| | Monday | Tuesday | Wednesday | Thursday | Friday |
| This week | Rachel | Dora | Adam | Dora | Adam |
| Next week | Adam | Dora | Rachel | Dora | Adam |

1. Dora eats lunch at her desk on Tuesday __*and*__ Thursday.

2. On Monday, Rachel _____ Adam answer calls.

3. This week, Adam eats lunch at his desk on Wednesday _____ Friday.

4. Dora and Adam eat lunch at their desks twice a week, _____

   Rachel doesn't. She eats lunch at her desk only once a week.

Check your answers. See page 136.

**1** Read the questions. Look at the letter of recommendation. Complete the sentences.

---

## WESTPORT COMMUNITY COLLEGE                    WCC

**May 25, 2009**

To Whom It May Concern:

I am happy to write this letter of recommendation for Federico Robles. Federico is a student in the Dental Assistant Certificate Program here at WCC. He will graduate in June.

Federico is an excellent student and a hard worker. He can manage a dental office, schedule appointments, and take care of patient records. He can assist dentists with many duties.

I recommend Federico very highly. He will be an excellent dental assistant. Please contact me for more information.

Sincerely,

*Carrie McIntosh*
Carrie McIntosh, Instructor

---

1. Carrie McIntosh is Federico's ____ .
   a. boss
   b. dental assistant
   c. instructor

2. This letter of recommendation is about ____ .
   a. Carrie McIntosh
   b. Federico
   c. Federico's new boss

3. Federico can ____ .
   a. manage a dental office
   b. schedule appointments
   c. both a and b

4. Federico ____ .
   a. is looking for a job
   b. is going to start school
   c. has a job now

5. In June, Federico is going to ____ .
   a. get a new job
   b. graduate
   c. quit his job

6. In this program, Federico learned to ____ .
   a. assist dentists
   b. take care of patients
   c. teach dental assistants

**2** Answer the questions.

1. Who wrote the letter? *Carrie McIntosh wrote the letter.*

2. When did she write the letter? _____

3. Where does she teach? _____

4. What program does she teach in? _____

5. What job skills did Federico learn? List them. _____

_____

Check your answers. See page 136.

## 3 Match the jobs with the pictures.

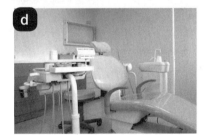

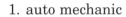

1. auto mechanic
2. orderly
3. housewife
4. cashier
5. construction worker
6. dental assistant
7. gas station attendant
8. teacher

## 4 Complete the sentences. Use the jobs from Exercise 3.

1. A _____ *housewife* _____ takes care of a family.

2. A _____ operates large machines.

3. An _____ helps the nurses.

4. A _____ assists the dentist.

5. An _____ repairs cars.

6. A _____ teaches students.

7. A _____ handles money.

8. A _____ pumps gas.

*Check your answers. See page 137.*

**1** Read Michael's employment history. Complete the sentences. Use the correct form of the verb.

---

**Employment History: Michael Bitter**

Michael Bitter is a dental assistant. He _____*works*_____ at Dr. White's Dental Clinic. He started
                1. work

in 2005. He _____ appointments for patients. He _____ the phones and
           2. make                                  3. answer

_____ messages. He _____ the patients and _____
   4. take                         5. prepare                      6. assist
the dentist.

From 1991 to 2003, Michael _____ at Freshie's Pizza. He had two jobs there.
                                     7. work

From 1999 to 2003, he _____ a cashier. He _____ money and
                      8. be                        9. handle

_____ the credit card machine. From 1991 to 1999, he _____ a busboy.
 10. operate                                             11. be

Michael _____ to Westport Community College from 2003 to 2005. He
           12. go

_____ a full-time student in the Dental Assistant Certificate Program. He _____
  13. be                                             14. graduate

in June 2005. In June 2000, he _____ his GED at Staples Adult School.
                                  15. get

---

**2** Answer the questions. Use the employment history in Exercise 1.

1. When did Michael start his job at the dental clinic?

   *He started his job at the dental clinic in 2005.*

2. Where did he work for 12 years?

   _____

3. What did he do from 2003 to 2005?

   _____

4. Where did he study for his GED?

   _____

5. When did he get his GED?

   _____

6. Where does he work now?

   _____

*Check your answers. See page 137.*

**3** Rewrite the sentences. Use the simple past.

1. I prepare food, but I don't clear the tables.

   *I prepared food, but I didn't clear the tables.*

2. I handle money and talk to people every day.

   _____

3. I help the nurses, but I don't help the doctors.

   _____

4. I take care of my children and my house.

   _____

5. I pump gas and check the engines, but I don't repair cars.

   _____

6. I operate large machines and build houses.

   _____

**4** Match the pictures with the sentences in Exercise 3. Then write the words.

| cashier | construction worker | housewife |
|---------|--------------------|-----------| 
| chef | gas station attendant | orderly |

a. _____

_____

b. _1_

_____ *chef* _____

c. _____

_____

d. _____

_____

e. _____

_____

f. _____

_____

Check your answers. See page 137.

# *Another view*

## 1 Read the job ads. Write the words. Start each word with a capital letter.

| auto mechanic | busboy | cashier | construction worker | dental assistant | orderly |

**1.** _____*Orderly*_____ Needed. Help patients walk, take patients for X-rays, deliver X-rays and mail, help nurses, talk to patients. No experience necessary.

**4.** _____ Wanted. Dental office needs friendly worker. Assist dentist and take care of office. Experience or Dental Assistant Certificate needed.

**2.** _____ Wanted. You will need to handle money, use a cash register, know basic math, be friendly with customers, and be on time. Restaurant experience necessary.

**5.** _____ Needed. *Busy car repair shop needs worker. Experience with American and foreign cars useful. Five years of experience necessary.*

**3.** _____ Needed. You need to have 2 years of experience building houses. Need a driver's license. Need to be able to work alone.

**6.** _____ Wanted. New restaurant needs worker to clear and clean tables. No experience necessary. Need to work fast.

## 2 Read the sentences. Which job is best for each person? Write the jobs from Exercise 1.

1. I am friendly and like to help people. _____*orderly*_____
2. I like to use tools and machines. _____C w.._____
3. I can handle money, and I like math. _____Cashier_____
4. I repaired cars for se en years. _____.on._____
5. I cleared tables in a restaurant last year. _____b b._____
. I like to work alone. _____C w._____
7. I ha e a Dental Assistant Certificate. _____d.a._____
8. I can work fast. _____b b._____

*Check your answers. See page 137.*

**3** Read the questions. Look at Freda's employment history.
Circle the answers.

**Employment History: Freda Forsyth**

Freda Forsyth is a salesperson. She works at
The Corner Mart. She started in 2002. She helps
the customers, handles money, and cleans the store.
She also delivers groceries to people's houses. She
likes this job very much.

From 2000 to 2001, Freda was a gas station
attendant. She worked at a gas station called Gasco.
She pumped gas and checked car engines. She also
handled money. She wasn't happy in this job.

Freda's first job was at Cottage Hospital. She
was an orderly. She worked there from 1995 to
1999. She assisted the nurses and helped the
patients. She liked the people, but she didn't like
her schedule. She often worked the night shift.

1. What was Freda's first job?
   a. an orderly
   b. a gas station attendant
   c. a salesperson

2. How long did Freda work at Cottage Hospital?
   a. one year
   b. four years
   c. seven years

3. What did she like about her job as an orderly?
   a. the food
   b. the night shift
   c. the people

4. What did Freda do at Gasco?
   a. She prepared food.
   b. She pumped gas.
   c. She repaired cars.

5. Where does Freda work now?
   a. The Corner Mart
   b. Gasco
   c. Cottage Hospital

6. Which job does Freda like the best?
   a. her first job
   b. her second job
   c. her job now

Check your answers. See page 137.

**Daily living**

**1** Look at the picture. Write the words.

| dishwasher | garbage | lightbulb | sink |
|---|---|---|---|
| dryer | leak | lock | washing machine |

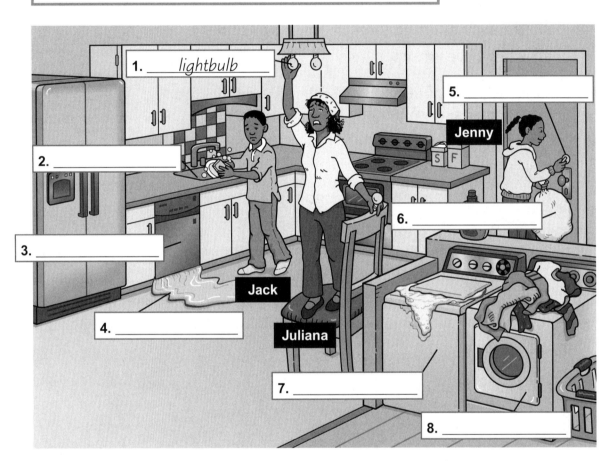

1. _____*lightbulb*_____

5. _____

Jenny

2. _____

6. _____

Jack

3. _____

4. _____

Juliana

7. _____

8. _____

**2** Complete the sentences. Use the words from Exercise 1.

1. Jenny is taking out the _____*garbage*_____ .

2. She is unlocking the door. Her hand is on the _____ .

3. Juliana is changing a _____ .

4. Jack is washing the dishes in the _____ .

5. There is water on the floor in front of the _____ .

6. The dishwasher has a _____ .

7. There is soapy water coming from the _____ .

8. There are clothes on top of the _____ .

*Check your answers. See page 137.*

**3** Look at the picture in Exercise 1. Answer the questions.

1. How many appliances does Juliana have in her kitchen?

*She has five appliances in her kitchen.*

2. Which appliances does she have?

_____

3. How many appliances have problems?

_____

4. Which appliances have problems?

_____

**4** Read the ad. Write the words.

| dishwasher | dryer | lightbulbs | lock | sink | washing machine |

**Seals**

## HUGE KITCHEN APPLIANCE SALE
### WASHING MACHINES! DRYERS! DISHWASHERS!
### THURSDAY–SUNDAY.  FREE DELIVERY!

**Make the day shine!**

4 FOR $10

1. ___*lightbulbs*___

**Keep your office safe!**

$30

2. _____

**Make your bathroom special!**

$200

3. _____

**Make dinner cleanup easy!**

$600

4. _____

**Get those stains out! Dry laundry quickly!**

$800          $700

5. _____

6. _____

Check your answers. See page 137.

*Study the chart on page 123.*

**1** Complete each question with *do* or *does*. Then write the answer.

1. Which plumber ___do___ they recommend?

   (Jerry's Plumbing) _They recommend Jerry's Plumbing._

2. Which teacher _____ he recommend?

   (Joe Thompson) _____

3. Which electrician _____ you recommend?

   (Wired Electric) _____

4. Which drugstore _____ they recommend?

   (Rite Price) _____

5. Which bank _____ she recommend?

   (Bank and Trust) _____

6. Which supermarket _____ he recommend?

   (SaveMore) _____

**2** Answer the questions. Use the words in parentheses.

1. Which babysitter does Marian recommend?

   (her cousin) _Marian recommends her cousin._____

2. Which plumber do you suggest?

   (Drains R Us) _____

3. Which auto mechanic does your husband like?

   (Ed Peterson) _____

4. Which doctor does your daughter recommend?

   (Dr. White) _____

5. Which supermarket do you and your family like?

   (Food City) _____

6. Which ESL program does your wife recommend?

   (Rockland Adult School) _____

7. Which clinic do you and your husband suggest?

   (the City Clinic) _____

**Check your answers. See page 137.**

**3** Read the ads. Circle the answers.

1. It's Saturday, and your friend's dishwasher has a leak.

   You recommend **Fix It** /(**ABC**)

2. You want a licensed repair person to fix your dryer.

   Your friend recommends **Fix It** / **ABC**.

3. Your mother needs a repair person for her stove right now.

   You recommend **Fix It** / **ABC**.

4. You want the repair person to clean the floor after the job is finished.

   Your parents recommend **Fix It** / **ABC**.

**4** Read the ads. Write the answers. Give reasons.

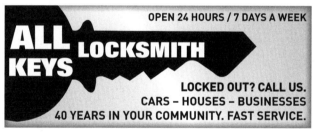

1. Which locksmith do you recommend?

   (All Keys / 24 hours) _I recommend All Keys. It's open 24 hours._

2. Which locksmith do they suggest?

   (Smitty's / licensed) _____

3. Which locksmith does Harry like?

   (All Keys / more experienced) _____

4. Which locksmith does Muriel suggest?

   (Smitty's / free keys) _____

5. Which locksmith do the Corwins recommend?

   (All Keys / fast service) _____

*Check your answers. See page 137.*

# *Can you call a plumber, please?*

*Study the chart on page 126.*

**1** Rewrite the questions. Use the words in parentheses.

1. Can you call a plumber, please?

   (Could) *Could you call a plumber, please?*

2. Could you change the lightbulb, please?

   (Would) _____

3. Would you fix the lock, please?

   (Will) _____

4. Could you fix the dryer, please?

   (Would) _____

5. Would you unclog the sink, please?

   (Could) _____

6. Would you fix the leak, please?

   (Can) _____

**2** Circle the correct answers.

1. Could you recommend a bank?
   a. Yes, maybe later.
   b. Yes, of course.

2. Would you repair the dishwasher?
   a. Sorry, I can't right now.
   b. Sorry, I'd be happy to.

3. Can you suggest a good doctor?
   a. No, of course.
   b. Yes, I'd be happy to.

4. Will you fix the lock now, please?
   a. No, not now. Maybe later.
   b. No, I'd be happy to.

5. Could you call an electrician now, please?
   a. Sure. Maybe later.
   b. Yes, of course.

6. Would you repair the toilet now, please?
   a. No, I can right now.
   b. Sorry, I can't right now.

*Check your answers. See page 138.*

**3** Look at the picture. Make requests for the landlord.

1. **A** _Could you fix the window, please?_
   (Could / fix / window)
   **B** Sure, I'd be happy to.

2. **A** _____
   (Would / repair / refrigerator)
   **B** No, not now.  aybe later.

3. **A** _____
   (Can / fix / light)
   **B** Yes, of course.

4. **A** _____
   (Will / unclog / sink)
   **B** Sorry, I can't right now.

5. **A** _____
   (Could / change / lock)
   **B** No, not now.  aybe later.

. **A** _____
   (Would / fix / dishwasher)
   **B** Sure, I'd be happy to.

**4** Read the list. Make requests. Use *Could*.

1. **A** _Could you fix the light, please?_
   **B** No, maybe later.

2. **A** _____
   **B** Yes, of course.

3. **A** _____
   **B** Sorry, I can't right now.

4. **A** _____
   **B** Sure. I'd be happy to.

5. **A** _____
   **B** Yes, of course.

. **A** _____
   **B** No, maybe later.

1. fix the light
2. unclog the bathtub
3. change the lightbulb
4. repair the dishwasher
5. clean the bathroom
6. call a plumber

*Check your answers. See page 138.*

**1** Read the questions. Read Rico's e-mail about his new apartment. Circle the answers.

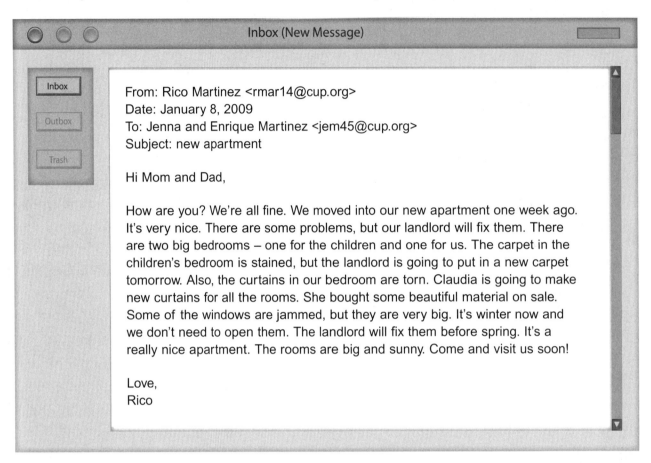

From: Rico Martinez <rmar14@cup.org>
Date: January 8, 2009
To: Jenna and Enrique Martinez <jem45@cup.org>
Subject: new apartment

Hi Mom and Dad,

How are you? We're all fine. We moved into our new apartment one week ago. It's very nice. There are some problems, but our landlord will fix them. There are two big bedrooms – one for the children and one for us. The carpet in the children's bedroom is stained, but the landlord is going to put in a new carpet tomorrow. Also, the curtains in our bedroom are torn. Claudia is going to make new curtains for all the rooms. She bought some beautiful material on sale. Some of the windows are jammed, but they are very big. It's winter now and we don't need to open them. The landlord will fix them before spring. It's a really nice apartment. The rooms are big and sunny. Come and visit us soon!

Love,
Rico

1. What is the landlord going to do tomorrow?
   a. fix the windows
   b. put in a new carpet
   c. repair the curtains

2. What is Claudia going to do?
   a. fix the curtains
   b. make new curtains
   c. wash the curtains

3. Rico is not upset about the jammed windows. Why?
   a. because it's cold outside
   b. because it's hot outside
   c. because the landlord will fix them tomorrow

4. What is the problem in the children's bedroom?
   a. The windows are broken.
   b. The curtains are torn.
   c. The carpet is stained.

5. Why does Rico like the windows?
   a. They are new.
   b. They are big.
   c. They are not cracked.

6. What does Rico like about the apartment?
   a. It's sunny and the rooms are big.
   b. The landlord is nice.
   c. The curtains are beautiful.

*Check your answers. See page 138.*

**2** Look at the picture. Write the words.

| bent | cracked | scratched |
| broken | dripping | stained |
| burned out | jammed | torn |

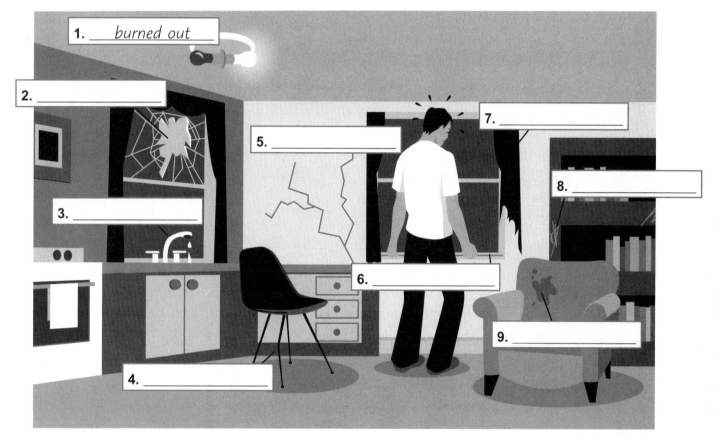

1. _burned out_
2. _____
3. _____
4. _____
5. _____
6. _____
7. _____
8. _____
9. _____

**3** Complete the sentences. Use words from Exercise 1.

1. One window won't open. It's _____jammed_____ .

2. The other window is _____ .

3. One lightbulb is _____ .

4. The faucet in the kitchen is _____ .

5. The curtain is _____ .

6. The wall is _____ .

7. The chair has a _____ leg.

8. The bookcase is _____ .

Check your answers. See page 138.

**1** Read the letter. Write the words.

| | | | |
|---|---|---|---|
| broken | clogged | dripping | scratched |
| burned out | cracked | jammed | stained |

December 2, 2009

Dear Ms. Torrant,

We are tenants in your apartment building. We are writing this letter because we are upset about problems in the building.

There are ___broken___ windows and many _____ ceilings.
      1.                        2.
You need to paint the walls because they are _____ . We can't open some
                    3.
windows because they are _____ . You need to replace many of the
                4.
lightbulbs in the halls because they are _____ . Some faucets in the
                  5.
sinks are _____ . Also, many doors are _____ and some
      6.                    7.
toilets are _____ .
      8.

Please reply to Jim Bowen in Apartment 822. Thank you for your attention.

Sincerely,

The tenants of 616 State Street

*Sharmin Patel* Apt. 201    *Randy Jones* Apt. 412    *Brad Wilson* Apt. 605

**2** Answer the questions. Use the information in Exercise 1.

1. How many signatures can you see? _Three signatures._____

2. List all the apartment numbers in the letter. _____

3. What is the date of this letter? _____

4. Who is the letter to? _____

5. What is the closing of the letter? _____

6. How many paragraphs are there in the body of the letter? _____

7. Who should Ms. Torrant reply to? _____

**Check your answers. See page 138.**

**3** Read the list of problems. Complete the letter of complaint.

```
List of Problems for:
78 Hillspoint Road Apartments

Apartment        Problem
4B               Leaking dishwasher
6A               Stained carpet
1B               Cracked bathtub
2C               Clogged toilet
3A               Broken stove
```

July 3, 2009

Dear Mr. Treelake,

I am a tenant in your apartment building at 78 Hillspoint Road. I am writing to you about some problems in the apartments.

Apartment 1B has a ___*cracked bathtub*___ . The _____ in
                                        1.                          2.

Apartment 4B is _____ . The tenants in Apartment 2C have a
                          3.

_____ . Could you please call a plumber to fix these three
                4.

problems?

Also, the _____ in Apartment 3A is _____ .
                     5.                      6.

The tenants can't use it. Would you please call a repair person?

The _____ in Apartment 6A is _____ . You
               7.                      8.

need to clean it.

You need to fix these problems right away. Your tenants are upset. Please call me at (825) 555-1574. Thank you for your attention.

Sincerely,

*C. M. Valdez*
Claire Valdez
Apartment 5C

Check your answers. See page 138.

**1** Read the questions. Look at the invoice. Circle the answers.

**Travis Carpet Cleaning**

4830 Avenue Montague
Montreal, Canada H4L 3Y2
(514) 555-5432 FAX: (514) 555-5433

Commercial and Residential
**We keep you clean!**

Invoice # 5554

Date : 4/16/09

Technician : Lisa Travis

Payment: ☐ cash ☒ check ☐ credit card

Customer : Mikey Morin

Customer address : 42 Avenue Brentwood, Montreal

Customer telephone : (514) 555 5952

| Description of work | Amount |
|---|---|
| 1. Clean dirty carpet in living room, bedroom, and hall | $54.95 (three-room special) |
| 2. Clean dirty carpet in extra bedroom | $35.50 |
| 3. Extra work on stained carpet in hall | $15.00 |

**Total: $105.45**

1. How much was the three-room special?
   a. $15.00
   b. $35.50
   c. $54.95
   d. $105.45

2. Where was the stained carpet?
   a. in the hall
   b. in the bedroom
   c. in the extra bedroom
   d. in the living room

3. How much is the total?
   a. $35.50
   b. $89.55
   c. $105.45
   d. $110.45

4. Who is the customer?
   a. Lisa Travis
   b. Mikey Morin
   c. Montague
   d. Travis Carpet Cleaning

5. How did the customer pay?
   a. with cash
   b. by check
   c. by credit card
   d. none of the above

6. What is the customer's telephone number?
   a. (514) 555-5432
   b. (514) 555-5433
   c. (514) 555-5554
   d. (514) 555-5952

*Check your answers. See page 138.*

**2** Complete the chart. Use the repair people and problems in the box. People can be used more than once.

| Problems | | Repair people | |
|---|---|---|---|
| a leaking sink | a broken lock | a carpenter | a locksmith    a plumber |
| burned-out lights | a stained carpet | a painter | an appliance repair person |

**Who fixes what?**

| Problem | Repair person |
|---|---|
| 1. a clogged sink | 1. *a plumber* |
| 2. | 2. a carpet cleaner |
| 3. | 3. an electrician |
| 4. a jammed key | 4. |
| 5. an overflowing toilet | 5. |
| 6. | 6. a plumber |
| 7. | 7. a locksmith |
| 8. stained walls | 8. |
| 9. a leaking dishwasher | 9. |
| 10. a broken chair | 10. |

**3** Complete the sentences.

| | | | |
|---|---|---|---|
| bent key | burned-out lightbulb | cracked window | jammed window |
| broken lock | clogged sink | dripping faucet | stained carpet |

1. I can't unlock my door. My key is not working. I have a _____ *bent key* _____ .

2. The water in my sink won't go down the drain. I have a _____ .

3. It's very dark in the hall. I can't turn on the light. I have a _____ .

4. It's hot, but I can't open my window. I have a _____ .

5. I can't sleep because there's a noise from my sink. I have a _____ .

6. My son spilled milk on the floor in the living room. I have a _____ .

7. I can't lock the door. I have a _____ .

8. I can't open the window because the glass will fall out. I have a _____ .

Check your answers. See page 138.

**1** Look at the picture. Write the words.

| | | | |
|---|---|---|---|
| balloons | a card | a guest | a piece of cake |
| a cake | flowers | perfume | a present |

1. _balloons_

3. _____

5. _____

7. _____

2. _____

4. _____

6. _____

8. _____

**2** Find the words.

| | |
|---|---|
| balloons | |
| cake | |
| card | |
| flowers | |
| graduation | |
| guest | |
| party | |
| perfume | |
| piece | |
| present | |

```
g  p  a  r  t  y  p  p  p
r  r  e  t  a  e  g  s  i
a  e  p  a  y  u  u  b  e
d  s  i  c  g  p  e  a  c
u  e  c  a  k  e  s  l  e
a  n  b  r  s  r  t  l  p
t  t  n  d  a  f  i  o  a
i  e  r  f  s  u  n  o  f
o  u  c  y  l  m  t  n  t
n  f  l  o  w  e  r  s  a
```

*Check your answers. See page 138.*

**3** Read the list of things to do. Circle the answers.

## To-do list for Lee's Graduation Party – Saturday, June 23

| Tasks | Who | Done |
|---|---|---|
| invite guests | Lee | ✓ |
| make a chocolate cake | Marsha | |
| buy balloons | Bill | ✓ |
| cut some flowers | Sandy | |
| buy "Rose Petal" perfume | Bill | ✓ |
| buy a card | Marsha | ✓ |
| sign the card | Bill, Evan, Sandy, Marsha | |
| shop for party food | Evan | ✓ |
| cook the food | Sandy, Marsha | |
| clean the house | Bill, Evan, Sandy, Marsha | |

1. What kind of party is it?
   a. birthday
   (b) graduation
   c. wedding

2. How many tasks does Lee have?
   a. 1
   b. 2
   c. 3

3. Who is going to make a cake?
   a. Lee
   b. Marsha
   c. Sandy

4. What did Bill buy?
   a. balloons and perfume
   b. a graduation cake and party food
   c. a present and a card

5. Who is going to clean the house?
   a. Bill, Evan, Sandy, and Marsha
   b. Bill, Evan, Sandy, Marsha, and Lee
   c. Lee

6. Which task is done?
   a. the cleaning
   b. the cooking
   c. the shopping

7. Who is going to cut the flowers?
   a. Bill
   b. Evan
   c. Sandy

8. Who shopped for party food?
   a. Bill
   b. Evan
   c. Sandy

Check your answers. See page 138.

# *Would you like some cake?*

*Study the chart on page 126.*

## 1 Read the answers. Write the questions.

1. **A** <u>Would you like some cake?</u>
   some cake

   **B** Yes, I would.

2. **A** _____
   some coffee

   **B** Yes, they would.

3. **A** _____
   some ice cream

   **B** Yes, we would.

4. **A** _____
   a balloon

   **B** Yes, she would.

5. **A** _____
   some flowers

   **B** Yes, they would.

6. **A** _____
   some dessert

   **B** Yes, I would.

7. **A** _____
   a cup of tea

   **B** Yes, he would.

## 2 Read the questions. Circle the answers.

1. **A** Would you like some cake?
   **B** (a.) Yes, I would.
      b. I'd like some cake.

2. **A** What would you like?
   **B** a. Yes, please.
      b. I'd like some coffee, please.

3. **A** Would they like a cup of tea?
   **B** a. No, they wouldn't.
      b. No, I'd not.

4. **A** What would she like?
   **B** a. She'd like it.
      b. She'd like a sandwich.

5. **A** Would they like some ice cream?
   **B** a. Yes, they would.
      b. They would like some soda.

6. **A** What would he like to drink?
   **B** a. He'd like some soda, please.
      b. Yes, he would.

7. **A** Would you like some coffee?
   **B** a. He'd like water and I'd like tea.
      b. Yes, we would.

8. **A** What would you like to eat?
   **B** a. No, thanks.
      b. I'd like a piece of cake.

*Check your answers. See page 138.*

**3** Look at the pictures. Complete the conversations.

1. **A** What would your friends like to drink?

   **B** *They'd like some soda.*

2. **A** Would your husband like something to drink?

   **B** Yes, please. _____

3. **A** What would you and your husband like to eat?

   **B** _____

4. **A** Would your daughter like a sandwich?

   **B** No, thanks. But _____ .

5. **A** Would you like something to eat?

   **B** Yes, please. _____

6. **A** Would you like something to drink?

   **B** No, thanks. But _____ .

**4** Complete the conversation. Write the words.

**Larry** Susie and Jerry! Welcome to Sarah's graduation party!

            *What would you*  like to drink?
                  1.

**Susie** _____ some soda, please.
          2.

**Larry** _____ a piece of cake, too?
          3.

**Susie** No, _____ . I'm full.
          4.

**Larry** OK. How about you, Jerry? _____ something to drink?
                            5.

**Jerry** Yes, _____ . I'm very thirsty.
          6.

**Larry** OK. _____ some soda?
          7.

**Jerry** No, thanks. _____ a cup of tea, please.
          8.

**Larry** OK. Here you go. _____ something to eat?
          9.

**Jerry** Yes, please. _____ a hot dog, a sandwich, some
          10.

cookies, and two pieces of cake.

**Larry** Wow! OK. How about your children? _____ like to eat?
                  11.

**Jerry** My children? This food is for them!

Check your answers. See page 138.

# *Tim gave Mary a present.*

*Study the chart on page 126.*

**1** Rewrite the sentences.

1. Tim gave a present to Mary.

   *Tim gave Mary a present.*

2. Jim brought some flowers to Sarah.

   _____

3. Elias wrote an e-mail to his father.

   _____

4. Marta bought some soda for her son.

   _____

5. Felix gave some ice cream to his children.

   _____

6. Liu Na sent a birthday card to her mother.

   _____

**2** Answer the questions. Use *her*, *him*, or *them* in the answers. Use the information in Exercise 1.

1. **A** What did Tim give Mary?

   **B** *Tim gave her a present.*

2. **A** What did Jim bring Sarah?

   **B** _____

3. **A** What did Elias write his father?

   **B** _____

4. **A** What did Marta buy her son?

   **B** _____

5. **A** What did Felix give his children?

   **B** _____

6. **A** What did Liu Na send her mother?

   **B** _____

*Check your answers. See page 139.*

**3** Read the list of Mick and Mina's wedding presents. Complete the conversation.

| Gift | From | Thank-you note |
|------|------|----------------|
| a check | Mina's parents | ✓ |
| a barbecue grill | Mick's brother | |
| a salad bowl | Maria | ✓ |
| coffee cups | Penny | |
| linens | Rod | |
| towels | Mina's sister | ✓ |

**Mick** Would you like some help?

**Mina** Yes, please. Could you write a thank-you note to your brother?

**Mick** OK. What did he give us?

**Mina** He gave us a ____barbecue grill____ .
                          1.

**Mick** Oh, that's right. OK. What about Maria? What did she give us?

**Mina** She gave us _____ . But don't write her a thank-you note
                           2.

because I already wrote one. Could you write Rod a note?

**Mick** Sure. Did he give us the _____ ?
                                        3.

**Mina** Yes. Did Penny give us the _____ ?
                                          4.

**Mick** Yeah. They're nice! And look, your parents gave us _____ .
                                                                  5.

**4** Answer the questions. Use the list in Exercise 3. Use *them*.

1. Who gave Mick and Mina a check?

   _Mina's parents gave them a check._

2. Who gave Mick and Mina coffee cups?

   _____

3. What did Maria give Mick and Mina?

   _____

4. What did Mina's sister give Mick and Mina?

   _____

5. What did Mina send her parents, her sister, and Maria?

   _____

Check your answers. See page 139.

# Lesson D  Reading

## 1  Read the e-mail. Answer the questions.

From: Do Cheon Yoon <dyoon13@cup.org>
Date: November 1, 2009
To: Chi Ho Yoon <chyoon42@cup.org>
Subject: Halloween

Hi Dad,
How are you? We're all great here. Last night was Halloween. Halloween is the children's favorite holiday. It was a lot of fun. The children made their own costumes. I took the children "trick-or-treating," and Yuni stayed home to give out candy. Over a hundred children came to our house for candy! After we got home, our children ate some candy, and then they went to bed. It will probably take about a month to eat all the candy!

Love,
Do Cheon

1. What is the children's favorite holiday? _Halloween._____

2. When was Halloween? _____

3. Who made the children's costumes? _____

4. Who went "trick-or-treating" with the children? _____

5. What did Yuni do? _____

6. How long will it take to eat all the candy? _____

## 2  Read the sentences. What was the celebration?

1. I wore a beautiful white dress. There were flowers everywhere.
   People gave us beautiful presents. _A wedding._____

2. We went to my grandmother's house. She cooked us a big
   turkey dinner. _____

3. The children went to all the houses in the neighborhood. The neighbors
   gave them candy. _____

4. Last Sunday, my children brought me breakfast in bed. They gave me
   presents, too. _____

5. We went to a big party. At midnight we celebrated. We went home
   at 1:00 a.m. _____

6. People gave us clothes and toys for our new baby. _____

Check your answers. See page 139.

**3** Match the celebrations with the items.

1. Thanksgiving _d_
2. a wedding ____
3. Valentine's Day ____
4. New Year's Eve ____
5. Mother's Day ____
6. a baby shower ____
7. a housewarming ____
8. Halloween ____
9. Independence Day ____

a. a white dress
b. presents for mothers
c. presents for a house
d. turkey for dinner
e. barbecues and fireworks
f. candy and costumes for children
g. parties until midnight
h. presents for babies
i. chocolates, flowers, and cards with red hearts

**4** Complete the chart. Use some celebrations more than once.

| a baby shower | Independence Day | New Year's Eve | Valentine's Day |
| a housewarming | Mother's Day | Thanksgiving | a wedding |

| Parties | No school or work | Give presents or cards |
|---|---|---|
| a baby shower | | a baby shower |
| | | |
| | | |
| | | |

Check your answers. See page 139.

**1** Write sentences.

1. the / for / interesting / you / Thank you / book / me / gave / .

   *Thank you for the interesting book you gave me.*

2. reading / excited / really / I'm / it / about / .

   _____

3. Thank you / for / cake / to / party / bringing / a / our / .

   _____

4. really / I / liked / a lot / it / .

   _____

5. to / coming / for / Thank you / my / party / graduation / .

   _____

6. you / hope / I / good / had / time / a / .

   _____

**2** Complete the thank-you note. Use the sentences from Exercise 1.

> June 15, 2009
>
> Dear Erica,
>
>     *Thank you for the interesting book you gave me* .
>                   1.
>
> _____ . It looks really
>            2.
>
> good.
>
>     Also, _____ .
>                  3.
>
> _____ . Chocolate is my favorite kind of
>     4.
>
> cake!
>
> _____ .
>          5.
>
> _____ . I had a very
>     6.
>
> good time! I hope to see you soon.
>
>              Love,
>              Joe

**Check your answers. See page 139.**

**3** Answer the questions. Use the information in Exercises 1 and 2.

1. Whose party was it?

   _It was Joe's party._

2. When did Joe write the thank-you note?

   _____

3. Who did Joe write the thank-you note to?

   _____

4. What did Erica give Joe?

   _____

5. What did Erica bring to the party?

   _____

6. Why did Joe like the cake?

   _____

**4** Read the story. Complete the thank-you note.

| chocolates | Dan | favorite | hope | Thank you | Valentine's Day |

> Dan visited Leanne on Valentine's Day. He gave Leanne a box of chocolates. They were Leanne's favorite kind of candy. She wrote him a note two days later.

February 16, 2009

Dear _____Dan_____ ,
    1.

Thank you for the _____ you gave me for _____ .
              2.                        3.

They were delicious! They were my _____ kind.
                                      4.

_____ so much for visiting me on Valentine's Day.
    5.

I _____ you had fun.
      6.

Love,
Leanne

Check your answers. See page 139.

## Lesson F Another view

**1** Read the questions. Look at the invitation. Circle the answers.

Inbox (New Message)

**A Day in the Park Barbecue**

RSVP BY APRIL 12

**Host:** Sheila Cristal
**Where:** Tucker's Grove Park
**When:** Saturday, April 15, 11:00–4:00
Come and celebrate **Paco's 18th birthday.**
Bring something to barbecue for lunch.
Children and pets welcome!

**Guest List**
How many people, as of April 14?
• YES 25   • NO 5   • MAYBE 0

to RSVP, CLICK HERE!

1. What is this?
   a. It's an e-mail invitation.
   b. It's an e-mail thank-you card.
   c. It's a paper invitation.
   d. It's an RSVP to an invitation.

2. When is the party?
   a. April 12
   b. April 14
   c. April 15
   d. April 18

3. What kind of party is it?
   a. a birthday party
   b. a children's party
   c. a graduation party
   d. a lunch party

4. How long is the party?
   a. four hours
   b. five hours
   c. six hours
   d. seven hours

5. How many guests are coming?
   a. 0
   b. 5
   c. 25
   d. 30

6. Who is giving the party?
   a. Cristal Sheila
   b. Paco Cristal
   c. Cristal Paco
   d. Sheila Cristal

7. What should people bring to the party?
   a. something to barbecue
   b. something to drink
   c. flowers and gifts
   d. all of the above

8. When do people need to say yes or no?
   a. by 4/12
   b. by 4/14
   c. by 4/15
   d. by 12/4

Check your answers. See page 139.

**2** Look at the pictures. Which activities are celebrations? Circle the letters.

**3** Complete the chart. Match the pictures in Exercise 2 with the celebrations.

| Letter | Celebration | Letter | Celebration |
|--------|-------------|--------|-------------|
| G | a baby shower | | Halloween |
| | a birthday party | | Independence Day |
| | a graduation | | a wedding |

Check your answers. See page 139.

# Reference charts

## Present continuous

### Wh- questions

| What | am | I | doing now? |
|------|-----|-----|------------|
| What | is<br>is<br>is | he<br>she<br>it | doing now? |
| What | are<br>are<br>are | we<br>you<br>they | doing now? |

### Affirmative statements

| I'm | working. |
|-----|----------|
| He's<br>She's<br>It's | working. |
| We're<br>You're<br>They're | working. |

| | | | |
|---|---|---|---|
| I'm | = I am | We're | = We are |
| He's | = He is | You're | = You are |
| She's | = She is | They're | = They are |
| It's | = It is | | |

## Simple present

### Wh- questions: What

| What | do | I<br>you<br>we<br>they | do every day? |
|------|------|------------------------|---------------|
| What | does | he<br>she<br>it | do every day? |

### Affirmative statements

| I<br>You<br>We<br>They | usually | work. |
|------------------------|---------|-------|
| He<br>She<br>It | usually | works. |

### Wh- questions: When

| When | do | I<br>you<br>we<br>they | usually work? |
|------|------|------------------------|---------------|
| When | does | he<br>she<br>it | usually work? |

### Affirmative statements

| I<br>You<br>We<br>They | usually | work | on Friday. |
|------------------------|---------|------|------------|
| He<br>She<br>It | usually | works | on Friday. |

# Simple present of *need* and *want*

## Wh- questions: *What*

| What | do | I you we they | want to do? need to do? |
|------|-----|----------------|--------------------------|
| What | does | he she it | want to do? need to do? |

## Affirmative statements

| I You We They | want need | to go. |
|----------------|------------|--------|
| He She It | wants needs | to go. |

# Simple present of *have to* + verb

## Wh- questions: *What*

| What | do | I you we they | have to do? |
|------|-----|----------------|-------------|
| What | does | he she it | have to do? |

## Affirmative statements

| I You We They | have to | go. |
|----------------|----------|-----|
| He She It | has to | go. |

# Simple present with *Which* questions

## Wh- questions: *Which*

| Which one | do | I you we they | recommend? |
|-----------|-----|----------------|------------|
| Which one | does | he she it | recommend? |

## Affirmative statements

| I You We They | recommend | Joe's Repair Shop. |
|----------------|-----------|---------------------|
| He She It | recommends | Joe's Repair Shop. |

# Simple past with regular and irregular verbs

## Wh- questions: What

| What | did | I you he she it we you they | do? |
|------|-----|------|-----|

## Affirmative statements

| I You He She It We You They | stayed. ate. |
|------|------|

## Negative statements

| I You He She It We You They | didn't | stay. eat. |
|------|------|------|

> didn't = did not

## Yes / No questions

| Did | I you he she it we you they | stay? eat? |
|-----|------|------|

## Short answers

| Yes, | I you he she it we you they | did. |
|------|------|------|

| No, | I you he she it we you they | didn't. |
|------|------|------|

## Wh- questions: When

| When | did | I you he she it we you they | move? leave? |
|------|-----|------|------|

## Affirmative statements

| I You He She It We You They | moved left | in July. last week. |
|------|------|------|

## Wh- questions: Where

| Where | did | I you he she it we you they | go? |
|-------|-----|------|-----|

## Affirmative statements

| I You He She It We You They | stayed went | home. |
|------|------|------|

# Future with *will*

### Wh- questions: What

| What | will | I<br>you<br>he<br>she<br>it<br>we<br>you<br>they | do | tomorrow? |
|------|------|--------------------------------|-----|-----------|

### Affirmative statements

| I'll<br>You'll<br>He'll<br>She'll<br>It'll<br>We'll<br>You'll<br>They'll | probably | work. |
|------|------|------|

'll = will

### Negative statements

| I<br>You<br>He<br>She<br>It<br>We<br>You<br>They | won't | work. |
|------|------|------|

won't = will not

# Should

### Wh- questions: What

| What | should | I<br>you<br>he<br>she<br>it<br>we<br>you<br>they | do? |
|------|--------|--------------------------------|-----|

### Affirmative statements

| I<br>You<br>He<br>She<br>It<br>We<br>You<br>They | should | work. |
|------|------|------|

### Negative statements

| I<br>You<br>He<br>She<br>It<br>We<br>You<br>They | shouldn't | work. |
|------|------|------|

shouldn't = should not

## Would you like . . . ?

### Yes / No questions

| Would | you he she we you they | like | some cake? |
|---|---|---|---|

### Short answers

| Yes, | I he she you we they | would. |
|---|---|---|

### Wh- questions: What

| What | would | you he she we you they | like? |
|---|---|---|---|

### Affirmative statements

| I'd He'd She'd You'd We'd They'd | like | some cake. |
|---|---|---|

'd = would

## Direct and indirect objects

| Tim gave a present to | Mary. me. you. him. her. it. us. you. them. |
|---|---|

| Tim gave | Mary me you him her it us you them | a present. |
|---|---|---|

# Comparative and superlative adjectives

| | Adjective | Comparative | Superlative |
|---|---|---|---|
| **Adjectives with one syllable** | cheap | cheaper | the cheapest |
| | large | larger | the largest |
| | long | longer | the longest |
| | new | newer | the newest |
| | nice | nicer | the nicest |
| | old | older | the oldest |
| | short | shorter | the shortest |
| | small | smaller | the smallest |
| | tall | taller | the tallest |
| | young | younger | the youngest |
| **Adjectives with one syllable ending in a vowel-consonant pair** | big | bigger | the biggest |
| | fat | fatter | the fattest |
| | hot | hotter | the hottest |
| | sad | sadder | the saddest |
| **Adjectives with two or more syllables** | beautiful | more beautiful | the most beautiful |
| | comfortable | more comfortable | the most comfortable |
| | crowded | more crowded | the most crowded |
| | expensive | more expensive | the most expensive |
| **Adjectives ending in -y** | friendly | friendlier | the friendliest |
| | heavy | heavier | the heaviest |
| | pretty | prettier | the prettiest |
| **Irregular adjectives** | good | better | the best |
| | bad | worse | the worst |

# Answer key

## Unit 1: Personal information

### Lesson A: Get ready

**Exercise 1** page 2

1. curly hair
2. short blond hair
3. a soccer uniform
4. straight hair
5. black shoes
6. striped pants
7. long black hair
8. a long skirt

**Exercise 2** page 2

1. curly hair
2. striped pants
3. short blond hair
4. a soccer uniform
5. straight hair
6. black shoes
7. long black hair
8. a long skirt

**Exercise 3** page 3

**Hair color**
black
blond
brown

**Hair length**
long
short

**Hair type**
curly
straight

**Exercise 4** page 3

1. She has long straight hair.
2. She has long curly hair.
3. He has short straight hair.
4. He has short curly hair.

### Lesson B: She's wearing a short plaid skirt.

**Exercise 1** page 4

1. a green and white striped dress
2. a black and blue checked shirt
3. a long blue coat
4. small red and yellow shoes
5. black plaid pants
6. short brown boots

**Exercise 2** page 4

1. a long blue coat
2. small red and yellow shoes
3. short brown boots
4. black plaid pants
5. a black and blue checked shirt
6. a green and white striped dress

**Exercise 3** page 5

1. a  2. c  3. b  4. c  5. a  6. b

**Exercise 4** page 5

**Colors**
black
green
purple
red

**Clothing**
coat
jeans
pants
sweater

**Sizes**
large
long
short
small

### Lesson C: What are you doing right now?

**Exercise 1** page 6

1. b  2. a  3. b  4. a  5. a  6. b

**Exercise 2** page 6

1A. do, do
1B. study
1A. are, doing
1B. am reading
2A. is, doing
2B. is, playing
2A. does, do
2B. plays
3A. does, do
3B. works
3A. is, doing
3B. is, watching
4A. does, do
4B. relaxes
4A. is, doing
4B. is, teaching

**Exercise 3** page 7

1. a  2. a  3. b  4. b  5. a  6. b

**Exercise 4** page 7

1. leaves      5. sits
2. goes        6. drinks
3. calls       7. studies
4. talk

**Exercise 5** page 7

1. is relaxing
2. is watching
3. are sitting
4. is drinking
5. is wearing
6. is speaking

### Lesson D: Reading

**Exercise 1** page 8

**Present continuous**
am writing
are working
am wearing

**Simple present**
think      go
miss       wears
is         goes

**Exercise 2** page 8

1. She's at the store in the lunchroom.
2. She lives in Chicago.
3. She lives in New York.
4. He wears a uniform.
5. She wears jeans.
6. She's writing an e-mail.

**Exercise 3** page 9

**Exercise 4** page 9

1. earrings
2. necklace
3. scarf
4. gloves
5. bracelet
6. purse
7. hat
8. tie
9. watch
10. ring

## Lesson E: Writing

**Exercise 1** page 10

**A**

1. green
2. goes
3. visits
4. watches
5. jacket
6. earrings
7. Norma

**B**

1. brown
2. white
3. jeans
4. goes
5. plays
6. Sarah

**C**

1. wearing
2. shoes
3. blond
4. blue
5. goes
6. studies
7. Martina

**Exercise 2** page 11

1. Bobby goes to New York City on the weekend.
2. Georgia is wearing a black scarf and a red coat.
3. Susana goes to work after school every Monday.
4. Mei's hair is long.
5. Martin is carrying his books in a backpack.
6. Christina is wearing a watch.

**Exercise 3** page 11

1. On the weekend, Mary teaches English.
2. Sam leaves early every night.
3. Alberto watches TV on Thursday.
4. On Saturday, Raquel plays volleyball.
5. Every Sunday, Michael wears a suit.
6. Petra has a birthday party every June.

## Lesson F: Another view

**Exercise 1** page 12

1. c  2. c  3. d  4. a  5. c  6. b

**Exercise 2** page 13

| Across | Down |
|--------|------|
| 1. purse | 2. shirt |
| 5. pants | 3. gloves |
| 6. earrings | 4. bracelet |
| 7. necklace | 8. coat |

**Exercise 3** page 13

1. earrings
2. coat
3. bracelet
4. pants
5. necklace
6. gloves
7. purse

# Unit 2: At school

## Lesson A: Get ready

**Exercise 1** page 14

1. a computer lab
2. a lab instructor
3. a monitor
4. a hall
5. a student
6. a mouse
7. a keyboard

**Exercise 2** page 14

1. keyboarding
2. instructor
3. computer
4. work
5. skill
6. register

**Exercise 3** page 15

1. Diego's English teacher.
2. Diego's computer lab instructor.
3. 555-23-0967.
4. Room H102.
5. 6:00–7:50 p.m.
6. Computer lab.

**Exercise 4** page 15

1. The lab instructor.
2. Computer monitors and keyboards.
3. Room C23-25.
4. Keyboarding, word processing, e-mailing, and using the Internet.
5. Room S210.
6. September 23.

## Lesson B: What do you want to do?

**Exercise 1** page 16

1. f  2. e  3. d  4. b  5. c  6. a

**Exercise 2** page 16

1. needs to take
2. wants to go
3. wants to get
4. want to talk
5. need to learn
6. need to register

**Exercise 3** page 17

1. He needs to take an auto mechanics class.
2. She needs to take a driver education class.
3. You need to take a citizenship class.
4. He needs to go to Room 131.
5. I need to go to Room 231.
6. They need to take a computer technology class.

## Lesson C: What will you do?

**Exercise 1** page 18

1. will
2. will
3. won't
4. will
5. won't
6. will

**Exercise 2** page 18

1. He'll work on Thursday.
2. He'll take a driving lesson on Tuesday.
3. He'll work on Friday.
4. He'll meet Lisa for lunch on Saturday.
5. He'll call Mom on Sunday.
6. He'll take an English class on Monday and Wednesday.

**Exercise 3** page 19

1. buy a house
2. go to the U.S.
3. open a business
4. study English
5. get a GED
6. study auto mechanics

**Exercise 4** page 19

1. What will she do in five years?
2. What will he do next year?
3. What will you do tomorrow?
4. What will they do this weekend?
5. What will you do in two years?
6. What will we do tonight?

## Lesson D: Reading

### Exercise 1 page 20

1. 18 months.
2. On March 14.
3. At City College.
4. Registration, the classes, and the certificate.
5. Teachers and current students.

### Exercise 2 page 20

1. b  2. c  3. c  4. a

### Exercise 3 page 21

1. e   3. a   5. c
2. d   4. f   6. b

### Exercise 4 page 21

1. nursing
2. culinary arts
3. accounting
4. automotive repair
5. hotel management
6. landscape design
7. computer technology
8. home health care

## Lesson E: Writing

### Exercise 1 page 22

1. b   3. f   5. c
2. d   4. a   6. e

### Exercise 2 page 22

1. get a second job on the weekend
2. he has a new baby
3. talk to people about job possibilities
4. read the classified section of the newspaper
5. look for jobs online
6. two months

### Exercise 3 page 23

1. goal
2. children
3. First
4. Second
5. Third
6. year

### Exercise 4 page 23

1. She wants to help her children with their homework.
2. She needs to find an adult school.
3. She needs to practice her English every day.
4. She needs to volunteer with the Parent-Teacher Association (PTA) at her children's school.
5. She will be ready next year.

## Lesson F: Another view

### Exercise 1 page 24

1. b   3. a   5. d
2. d   4. c   6. b

### Exercise 2 page 25

**Down**

1. culinary
2. hotel
3. landscape
4. home
5. computer

**Across**

6. automotive

# Unit 3: Friends and family

## Lesson A: Get ready

### Exercise 1 page 26

1. smoke
2. groceries
3. supermarket
4. engine
5. broken-down car
6. cell phone
7. trunk
8. hood

### Exercise 2 page 26

1. engine
2. smoke
3. hood
4. cell phone
5. supermarket
6. groceries
7. trunk
8. broken-down car

### Exercise 3 page 27

1. broke          5. smoke
2. supermarket    6. engine
3. groceries      7. hood
4. trunk

## Lesson B: What did you do last weekend?

### Exercise 1 page 28

1. b   3. b   5. a
2. a   4. b   6. a

### Exercise 2 page 28

1. barbecued      7. had
2. bought         8. listened
3. drove          9. met
4. ate            10. played
5. fixed          11. read
6. went           12. stayed

### Exercise 3 page 29

1. went
2. met
3. played
4. had
5. ate
6. drove

### Exercise 4 page 29

a. 5   b. 2   c. 3   d. 4   e. 1   f. 6

## Lesson C: When do you usually play soccer?

### Exercise 1 page 30

1. went
2. watch
3. cleaned
4. eats
5. leave
6. met

### Exercise 2 page 30

1. d   3. e   5. f   7. a
2. g   4. b   6. c   8. h

### Exercise 3 page 31

1. has      5. met
2. plays    6. gets
3. works    7. eat
4. has      8. ate

### Exercise 4 page 31

1. They usually buy groceries on Thursday.
2. She took her English exam on Friday.
3. He usually meets his friends after work.
4. She went to a movie with her uncle on Monday.
5. He met his friends at 5:30.
6. He studied for an English test.

## Lesson D: Reading

### Exercise 1 page 32

1. d   3. b   5. a   7. a
2. c   4. d   6. d   8. a

**Exercise 2** page 33

1. the laundry
2. the dishes
3. lunch
4. the bed
5. a bath
6. a nap
7. dressed
8. up

**Exercise 3** page 33

1. make
2. make
3. do
4. do
5. did
6. did
7. do
8. takes

## Lesson E: Writing

**Exercise 1** page 34

1. Ana usually gets up first.
2. Ron got up first this morning.
3. Ana usually gets the family up.
4. Ron got Ana up this morning.
5. Ana usually takes a bath every morning.
6. Ana didn't take a bath this morning.
7. Ed usually leaves for work at 7:20.

**Exercise 2** page 35

1. She gets dressed at 6:15.
2. She gets Sonia up at 6:30.
3. She eats her breakfast at 7:10.
4. She does the dishes at 7:45.
5. She checks the children's beds at 7:15.
6. She leaves the house at 7:55.

**Exercise 3** page 35

1. Next, First, Finally
2. Finally, First, Next

**Exercise 4** page 35

1. Last Monday, I had a very bad morning. First, I woke up late. Next, I didn't have time for breakfast. Finally, I was late for work.
2. Last Sunday, my family went to the beach. First, we had a picnic lunch. Next, we relaxed all afternoon. Finally, we drove home for dinner.

## Lesson F: Another view

**Exercise 1** page 36

1. c
2. d
3. a
4. b
5. c
6. d

**Exercise 2** page 37

1. plays volleyball, played soccer
2. goes to the movies, went to the mall
3. barbecue chicken, barbecued hamburgers
4. drives to the beach, drove to the mountains
5. cleans her apartment, cleaned her car

**Exercise 3** page 37

```
d  l  n  o  r  e  k  r  g  s  m  m
s  l  a  u  n  d  r  y  m  m  d  a
h  l  o  d  h  o  m  e  w  o  r  k
y  e  d  i  s  h  e  s  y  r  e  e
m  d  g  n  e  z  r  t  u  n  s  k
i  t  o  u  s  o  o  e  h  i  s  a
y  d  m  d  o  e  n  r  h  n  e  k
r  k  e  s  r  e  n  d  k  g  d  e
a  s  n  e  e  s  t  a  k  e  s  k
s  n  e  n  a  s  d  y  k  i  o  e
a  d  o  m  y  h  e  r  s  m  t  s
```

# Unit 4: Health

## Lesson A: Get ready

**Exercise 1** page 38

1. hand
2. crutches
3. accident
4. medicine
5. leg
6. headache
7. X-ray
8. hospital

**Exercise 2** page 38

1. hospital
2. X-ray
3. hand
4. headache
5. medicine
6. crutches
7. accident
8. leg

**Exercise 3** page 39

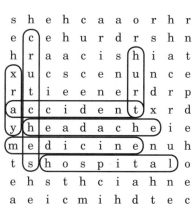

```
s  h  e  h  c  a  a  o  r  h  r
e  c  e  h  u  r  d  r  s  h  n
h  r  a  a  c  i  s  h  i  a  t
x  u  c  s  c  e  n  u  n  c  e
r  t  i  e  e  n  e  r  d  r  p
a  c  c  i  d  e  n  t  x  r  d
y  h  e  a  d  a  c  h  e  i  e
m  e  d  i  c  i  n  e  n  u  h
t  s  h  o  s  p  i  t  a  l  o
e  h  s  t  h  c  i  a  h  n  e
a  e  i  c  m  i  h  d  t  e  c
```

**Exercise 4** page 39

1. accident
2. hurt
3. hospital
4. X-ray
5. crutches
6. medicine
7. headache

**Exercise 4** page 39

1. She hurt her arm.
2. He hurt his leg.
3. He hurt his hand.

## Lesson B: What do I have to do?

**Exercise 1** page 40

1A. does, have to
1B. has to
2A. does, have to
2B. has to
3A. do, have to
3B. have to
4A. do, have to
4B. have to
5A. does, have to
5B. has to
6A. do, have to
6B. have to

**Exercise 2** page 40

1. He has to use crutches.
2. She has to see the doctor.
3. He has to get an X-ray.
4. He has to fill out an accident report.
5. She has to take medicine.
6. They have to go to the hospital.

**Exercise 3** page 41

1. c
2. f
3. d
4. e
5. b
6. a

**Exercise 4** page 41

1. prescription
2. do
3. have to
4. medicine
5. refrigerator
6. morning
7. food

## Lesson C: You should go to the hospital.

**Exercise 1** page 42

1. should
2. shouldn't
3. shouldn't
4. should
5. should
6. shouldn't

**Exercise 2 page 42**

1. shouldn't, should
2. shouldn't, should
3. should, shouldn't
4. shouldn't, should
5. should, shouldn't
6. should, shouldn't

**Exercise 3 page 43**

1. sprained ankle
2. accident
3. headache
4. medicine
5. stomachache
6. asthma

**Exercise 4 page 43**

1. should        4. should
2. shouldn't     5. should
3. should        6. shouldn't

**Lesson D: Reading**

**Exercise 1 page 44**

1. a  2. b  3. c  4. b  5. d  6. a

**Exercise 2 page 45**

1. d  2. e  3. b  4. a  5. c

**Exercise 3 page 45**

1. She has a rash.
2. They have allergies.
3. He has a swollen knee.
4. She has chest pains.
5. She has chills.
6. He has a sprained wrist.

**Exercise 4 page 45**

1. hurt
2. accident
3. chest
4. cut
5. medicine

**Lesson E: Writing**

**Exercise 1 page 46**

1. There were four accidents in August.
2. The waiter had a sprained ankle.
3. The cook burned his hand on August 10.
4. Mr. Engels cut his hand.
5. Ms. Perry had a sprained wrist.
6. The name of the restaurant is Sleepy Burgers.

**Exercise 2 page 46**

1. 3, 1, 2
2. 2, 1, 3

**Exercise 3 page 47**

1. burned      5. medicine
2. injuries    6. days
3. accident    7. shouldn't
4. has to      8. work

**Exercise 4 page 47**

1. Carlos Garcia was hurt.
2. He had burned hands.
3. He was hurt this afternoon / on May 9, 2007.
4. Yes, it was.
5. He can return to work on May 16, 2007.
6. The name of the restaurant is Fast Frank's Restaurant.

**Lesson F: Another view**

**Exercise 1 page 48**

1. c  2. c  3. d  4. c  5. b  6. a

**Exercise 2 page 48**

1. tablets
2. doctor
3. product
4. drowsiness

**Exercise 3 page 49**

| Across | Down |
| --- | --- |
| 1. prescription | 2. signature |
| 6. crutches | 3. hospital |
| 7. label | 4. doctor |
| 8. medicine | 5. tablet |

## Unit 5: Around town

**Lesson A: Get ready**

**Exercise 1 page 50**

1. a suitcase
2. an information desk
3. a waiting area
4. a track number
5. a ticket booth
6. a departure board

**Exercise 2 page 50**

1. a ticket booth
2. a suitcase
3. an information desk
4. a track number
5. a waiting area
6. a departure board

**Exercise 3 page 51**

1. a  2. f  3. d  4. c  5. b  6. e

**Exercise 4 page 51**

1. suitcase
2. train station
3. information desk
4. ticket booth
5. departure board
6. waiting area
7. track number

**Lesson B: How often? How long?**

**Exercise 1 page 52**

1. a    2. a    3. b    4. c

**Exercise 2 page 53**

1. f  2. a  3. b  4. e  5. d  6. c

**Exercise 3 page 53**

1. How often do you drive to the beach?
   How long does it take to drive to the beach?
2. How often do you walk to the park?
   How long does it take to walk to the park?
3. How often do you go downtown by bus?
   How long does it take to go downtown by bus?

**Lesson C: She often walks to school.**

**Exercise 1 page 54**

1. never
2. rarely
3. sometimes
4. often
5. always

**Exercise 2 page 54**

1. often        7. sometimes
2. rarely       8. sometimes
3. always       9. rarely
4. never       10. often
5. always      11. often
6. never       12. rarely

**Exercise 3 page 55**

1. He always walks to school.
2. He never drives to school.
3. He rarely eats lunch at 1:00 p.m.

4. He usually eats dinner at home.
5. He usually goes to sleep at 10:00 p.m.

## Exercise 4 page 55

| | |
|---|---|
| 1a. Yes | 3a. No |
| 1b. No | 3b. Yes |
| 2a. No | 4a. Yes |
| 2b. Yes | 4b. No |

## Lesson D: Reading

### Exercise 1 page 56

1. c   2. c   3. d   4. b

### Exercise 2 page 56

1. Mariam
2. at a hotel
3. know
4. Mariam

### Exercise 3 page 57

| | |
|---|---|
| 1. goes | 6. buy |
| 2. stays | 7. take |
| 3. takes | 8. write |
| 4. go | 9. stays |
| 5. go | |

### Exercise 4 page 57

6, 3, 2, 8, 5, 1, 7, 4

A How often do you go on vacation?
B I go on vacation once a year
A Where do you usually go?
B I usually go to Denver to see my parents.
A How long does it take to get there?
B It usually takes about three hours by plane.
A Do you always go by plane?
B Oh, yes! It takes two days by car.

## Lesson E: Writing

### Exercise 1 page 58

1. How often do trains go to Miami?
2. How long does it take to get to San Francisco?
3. How long does it take to drive to Detroit?
4. How often does the bus go to Boston?
5. How often do you visit your relatives in Houston?

6. Where do you usually stay?
7. What do you usually do there?

### Exercise 2 page 58

| | | | |
|---|---|---|---|
| a. 5 | c. 7 | e. 6 | g. 3 |
| b. 1 | d. 4 | f. 2 | |

### Exercise 4 page 59

1. Every year.
2. One week.
3. Rarely.
4. Very happy.

### Exercise 5 page 59

1. one hour and five minutes
2. one hour and forty-five minutes
3. nine minutes
4. one hour and seven minutes
5. half an hour (or 30 minutes)
6. one hour and twelve minutes

### Exercise 6 page 59

| | | | |
|---|---|---|---|
| 1. goes | | 7. uses | |
| 2. takes | | 8. sleeps | |
| 3. leaves | | 9. takes | |
| 4. gets | | 10. talks | |
| 5. doesn't like | | 11. likes | |
| 6. are | | 12. doesn't like | |

## Lesson F: Another view

### Exercise 1 page 60

1. How often does the bus go? It goes every half hour.
2. How does Shen Hui get to school?
   Shen Hui gets to school by bicycle.
3. How long does it take to get from Shen Hui's house to school by bicycle?
   It takes 20 minutes.
4. How often does Phillipe arrive on time?
   Phillipe always arrives on time.
5. How long does it take to get from Sara's house to school by subway?
   It takes 22 minutes.
6. How does Zoraida get to school?
   Zoraida drives to school.

### Exercise 2 page 61

1. Shen Hui
2. Zoraida
3. Phillipe

4. Mai
5. Sara

### Exercise 3 page 61

1. usually
2. always
3. rarely
4. sometimes
5. often
6. never

## Unit 6: Time

### Lesson A: Get ready

### Exercise 1 page 62

1. class picture
2. family
3. graduation
4. baby
5. photo album
6. wedding

### Exercise 2 page 62

1. photo album
2. graduation
3. family
4. wedding
5. class picture
6. baby

### Exercise 3 page 63

1. a   2. c   3. b   4. c   5. b

### Exercise 4 page 63

| | |
|---|---|
| 1. albums | 5. graduation |
| 2. pictures | 6. wedding |
| 3. baby | 7. family |
| 4. class | |

### Lesson B: When did you move here?

### Exercise 1 page 64

| | |
|---|---|
| 1. moved | 6. started |
| 2. had | 7. got |
| 3. began | 8. left |
| 4. studied | 9. met |
| 5. found | 10. graduated |

### Exercise 2 page 64

**Regular verbs**

moved
studied
started
graduated

**Irregular verbs**

had
began

found
got
left
met

**Exercise 3** page 64

1. I moved here in 2000.
2. Ken started college in September.
3. We met in 1988.
4. We got married in 1990.
5. They began taking English classes last year.
6. Norma left for vacation on Saturday.

**Exercise 4** page 65

1. When did Elsa meet Pablo?
2. When did they get married?
3. They had Gabriel in 1986.
4. When did they have Clara?
5. They left Guatemala in 1993.
6. They moved from Chicago to Detroit in 1995.
7. When did Elsa start taking ESL classes?
8. She got her driver's license in 2000.

**Lesson C: He graduated two years ago.**

**Exercise 1** page 66

**ago**
four days
a week
two years
a month
six months

**in**
December
1999
July
the afternoon
the morning

**on**
March 23rd
May 9th
Wednesday
April 11th, 1960
Saturday

**at**
6:15
night
noon
half past four

**Exercise 2** page 66

1. last
2. on
3. at
4. ago
5. in
6. this
7. before
8. on
9. before
10. ago

**Exercise 3** page 67

1. last
2. on
3. at
4. before
5. in
6. ago
7. after
8. last

**Exercise 4** page 67

1. He took his driving test four days ago.
2. He shopped for his sister's present last week.
3. He played basketball on Friday, May 15th.
4. He had a doctor's appointment at 4:30.
5. He took his books back to the library two days ago.

**Lesson D: Reading**

**Exercise 1** page 68

1. immigrated
2. worked
3. started
4. studied
5. began
6. met
7. fell
8. got
9. got
10. found
11. started
12. had
13. decided

**Exercise 2** page 68

1. She immigrated ten years ago.
2. She started English classes after she came to the U.S.
3. She studied English for three years.
4. They got married three years ago.
5. They found jobs after they got married.

**Exercise 3** page 69

a. 5  b. 3  c. 4  d. 1  e. 6  f. 2

**Exercise 4** page 69

1. immigrated
2. fell in love
3. got married
4. got engaged
5. got promoted
6. started a business
7. had a baby

8. retire
9. get a divorce

**Lesson E: Writing**

**Exercise 1** page 70

1. on
2. had
3. started
4. in
5. took
6. worked
7. In
8. learned
9. After
10. found
11. last
12. opened

**Exercise 2** page 70

1. b  2. d  3. f  4. a  5. c  6. e

**Exercise 3** page 71

1. On January 5, 1998, she left China.
   She left China on January 5, 1998.
2. In February 1998, she began English classes.
   She began English classes in February 1998.
3. For two years, she took English classes.
   She took English classes for two years.
4. In September 1999, she began vocational school.
   She began vocational school in September 1999.
5. In 2001, she graduated from vocational school.
   She graduated from vocational school in 2001.
6. In September 2001, she found a job as a chef.
   She found a job as a chef in 2001.
7. Last week, she opened her own restaurant.
   She opened her own restaurant last week.

**Lesson F: Another view**

**Exercise 1** page 72

1. b  2. a  3. b  4. a  5. c  6. d

**Exercise 2** page 73

1. a  2. f  3. b  4. e  5. d  6. c

**Exercise 3** page 73

1. stars in their eyes
2. popped the question
3. cold feet

4. tied the knot
5. smooth sailing
6. on the rocks

# Unit 7: Shopping

## Lesson A: Get ready

### Exercise 1 page 74

1. stove
2. salesperson
3. sofa
4. piano
5. customer
6. appliances
7. furniture
8. price tag

### Exercise 2 page 74

1. sofa
2. furniture
3. customer
4. stove
5. salesperson
6. price tag
7. piano
8. appliances

### Exercise 3 page 75

1. salesperson
2. customer
3. furniture
4. appliances
5. sofa
6. piano
7. stove
8. price tag

### Exercise 4 page 75

**Appliances**
piano
**Furniture**
car
**People**
price tag

## Lesson B: The brown sofa is bigger.

### Exercise 1 page 76

1. bigger
2. better
3. heavier
4. more comfortable

### Exercise 2 page 76

1. more comfortable
2. prettier
3. more expensive
4. cheaper
5. bigger
6. heavier

### Exercise 3 page 77

1. The dining room table is bigger.
2. The red chairs are smaller.
3. The refrigerator is more expensive.
4. The blue desk is older.
5. The green sofa is longer.
6. The black lamp is shorter.

## Lesson C: The yellow chair is the cheapest.

### Exercise 1 page 78

1. more expensive, the most expensive
2. cheaper, the cheapest
3. friendlier, the friendliest
4. better, the best
5. newer, the newest
6. heavier, the heaviest
7. lower, the lowest
8. more beautiful, the most beautiful
9. prettier, the prettiest
10. more crowded, the most crowded
11. more comfortable, the most comfortable
12. nicer, the nicest

### Exercise 2 page 78

1. the lowest
2. the most comfortable
3. the best
4. the most expensive
5. the nicest
6. the prettiest
7. the cheapest
8. the smallest
9. the most crowded
10. the heaviest

### Exercise 3 page 79

1. a small lamp, a smaller lamp, the smallest lamp
2. an expensive desk, a more expensive desk, the most expensive desk
3. a good TV, a better TV, the best TV

### Exercise 4 page 79

1. The evening skirt is the most expensive.
2. The evening skirt is the longest.
3. The jeans skirt is the cheapest.
4. The tennis skirt is the shortest.

## Lesson D: Reading

### Exercise 1 page 80

1. newest
2. big
3. best
4. beautiful
5. nicest
6. most expensive
7. oldest
8. cheaper
9. cheapest
10. small

### Exercise 2 page 80

1. The name of the store is Antique Alley.
2. It opened on May 1st.
3. The most expensive thing was a large mirror.
4. It was $1,300.
5. The cheapest thing was a small lamp.
6. It was $12.95.

### Exercise 3 page 81

**Down**
1. entertainment center
3. recliner
5. mirror
7. sofa bed
8. table

**Across**
2. furniture
4. china cabinet
6. dresser
9. bookcase

## Lesson E: Writing

### Exercise 1 page 82

1. The gift is for Miguel.
2. The gift is from his wife.
3. She gave him an airline ticket.
4. It's his 40th birthday.
5. He will go to Mexico City.
6. He will leave on August 10.

### Exercise 2 page 82

1. I bought the red sofa because it was the most comfortable.
2. Sandra gave her sister a pair of earrings because it was her birthday.
3. Mr. and Mrs. Chung shop at the Clothes Corner because it's the nicest store.
4. Roberto bought the brown recliner because it was on sale.
5. I bought an entertainment center because it was 50% off.

### Exercise 3 page 83

1. bigger
2. nicer
3. better
4. newer
5. more beautiful
6. higher
7. oldest
8. smallest
9. most crowded

### Exercise 4 page 83

1. Super Discounts, the smallest
2. Super Discounts, the oldest

3. Smart Department Store, the biggest
4. Smart Department Store, the most expensive
5. Best Discounts, the cheapest
6. Super Discounts, the most crowded

### Lesson F: Another view

**Exercise 1** page 84

1. c    3. a    5. c
2. d    4. a    6. b

**Exercise 2** page 85

1. You can get 50–80% off at Modern Furniture.
2. You can shop at 8:30 a.m. at Big Bill's Best Furniture.
3. Big Bill's Best Furniture has free delivery.
4. Modern Furniture sells only new furniture.
5. Nick's Nearly New is open seven days a week.

**Exercise 3** page 85

## Unit 8: Work

### Lesson A: Get ready

**Exercise 1** page 86

1. lab       5. linens
2. orderly     6. patient
3. co-workers   7. supplies
4. walker      8. wheelchair

**Exercise 2** page 86

1. lab       5. supplies
2. linens     6. patient
3. co-workers   7. walker
4. orderly     8. wheelchair

**Exercise 3** page 87

1. patient
2. co-workers
3. linens
4. wheelchair
5. orderly
6. walker

**Exercise 4** page 87

1. patient
2. supplies
3. linens
4. co-workers
5. lab
6. work

a. 4    c. 5    e. 6
b. 1    d. 3    f. 2

### Lesson B: Where did you go last night?

**Exercise 1** page 88

1. c    3. b    5. a    7. f
2. e    4. g    6. d

**Exercise 2** page 88

1. What
2. Where
3. What
4. What
5. Where
6. What

**Exercise 3** page 89

1A. What
1B. They met new patients in the reception area.
2A. Where
2B. She took her patient to the lab.
3A. What
3B. He picked up X-rays from the lab.
4A. What
4B. made the bed in Room 304, delivered X-rays to the doctors.
5A. Where
5B. Jorge went to Room 310.
6A. What
6B. He helped a patient.
7A. What
7B. She took patients from the lab to their rooms.
8A. Where
8B. She went to the fourth floor.
9A. What

9B. He prepared rooms on the second floor.
10A. Where
10B. They went to the cafeteria.

### Lesson C: I work on Saturdays and Sundays.

**Exercise 1** page 90

1. and    5. but
2. or     6. or
3. but    7. and
4. and    8. and

**Exercise 2** page 90

1. Jun eats lunch at noon or at 1:00.
2. Javier helps the nurses and the doctors.
3. Tien picks up the supplies at the warehouse, but she doesn't deliver them.
4. Rieko met her new co-workers this morning, but she didn't meet any patients.
5. At the restaurant, Mustafa made the soup and the salad.
6. Anatoly drinks coffee or tea.

**Exercise 3** page 91

1. Dora went to the meeting, but she didn't take notes.
2. Adam checked the office e-mail and went to the meeting.
3. Rachel prepared the meeting room, but she didn't make the coffee.
4. Dora and Adam went to the meeting, but they didn't prepare the meeting room.
5. Adam took notes and made copies.
6. Rachel picked up supplies and delivered the mail.

**Exercise 4** page 91

1. and
2. or
3. and
4. but

### Lesson D: Reading

**Exercise 1** page 92

1. c    3. c    5. b
2. b    4. a    6. a

**Exercise 2** page 92

1. Carrie McIntosh wrote the letter.

2. She wrote it on May 25, 2009.
3. She teaches at Westport Community College.
4. She teaches in the Dental Assistant Certificate Program.
5. manage a dental office, schedule appointments, and take care of patient records

### Exercise 3 page 93

1. e    3. c    5. b    7. g
2. h    4. a    4. a    8. f

### Exercise 4 page 93

1. housewife
2. construction worker
3. orderly
4. dental assistant
5. auto mechanic
6. teacher
7. cashier
8. gas station attendant

### Lesson E: Writing

#### Exercise 1 page 94

1. works     9. handled
2. makes     10. operated
3. answers    11. was
4. takes      12. went
5. prepares    13. was
6. assists     14. graduated
7. worked     15. got
8. was

#### Exercise 2 page 94

1. He started his job at the dental clinic in 2005.
2. He worked at Freshie's Pizza for 12 years.
3. He was a student from 2003 to 2005.
4. He studied for his GED at Staples Adult School.
5. He got his GED in June 2000.
6. He works at Dr. White's Dental Clinic now.

#### Exercise 3 page 95

1. I prepared food, but I didn't clear the tables.
2. I handled money and talked to people every day.
3. I helped the nurses, but I didn't help the doctors.
4. I took care of my children and my house.

5. I pumped gas and checked the engines, but I didn't repair cars.
6. I operated large machines and built houses.

#### Exercise 4 page 95

a. 3: orderly
b. 1: chef
c. 5: gas station attendant
d. 2: cashier
e. 6: construction worker
f. 4: housewife

### Lesson F: Another view

#### Exercise 1 page 96

1. Orderly
2. Cashier
3. Construction Worker
4. Dental Assistant
5. Auto Mechanic
6. Busboy

#### Exercise 2 page 96

1. orderly
2. construction worker
3. cashier
4. auto mechanic
5. busboy
6. construction worker
7. dental assistant
8. busboy

#### Exercise 3 page 97

1. a   2. b   3. c   4. b   5. a   6. c

## Unit 9: Daily living

### Lesson A: Get ready

#### Exercise 1 page 98

1. lightbulb
2. sink
3. dishwasher
4. leak
5. lock
6. garbage
7. washing machine
8. dryer

#### Exercise 2 page 98

1. garbage
2. lock
3. lightbulb
4. sink
5. dishwasher
6. leak

7. washing machine
8. dryer

### Exercise 3 page 99

1. She has five appliances in her kitchen.
2. She has a washing machine, a dryer, a stove, a refrigerator, and a dishwasher.
3. Two appliances have problems.
4. The dishwasher and the washing machine have problems.

### Exercise 4 page 99

1. lightbulbs
2. lock
3. sink
4. dishwasher
5. washing machine
6. dryer

### Lesson B: Which one do you recommend?

#### Exercise 1 page 100

1. do; They recommend Jerry's Plumbing.
2. does; He recommends Joe Thompson.
3. do; I recommend Wired Electric.
4. do; They recommend Rite Price.
5. does; She recommends Bank and Trust.
6. does; He recommends SaveMore.

#### Exercise 2 page 100

1. Marian recommends her cousin.
2. I suggest Drains R Us.
3. He likes Ed Peterson.
4. She recommends Dr. White.
5. We like Food City.
6. She recommends Rockland Adult School.
7. We suggest the City Clinic.

#### Exercise 3 page 101

1. ABC     3. Fix It
2. ABC     4. Fix It

#### Exercise 4 page 101

1. I recommend All Keys. It's open 24 hours.
2. They suggest Smitty's. It's licensed.

3. Harry likes All Keys. It's more experienced.
4. Muriel suggests Smitty's. It gives free keys.
5. They recommend All Keys. It has fast service.

### Lesson C: Can you call a plumber, please?

**Exercise 1 page 102**

1. Could you call a plumber, please?
2. Would you change the lightbulb, please?
3. Will you fix the lock, please?
4. Would you fix the dryer, please?
5. Could you unclog the sink, please?
6. Can you fix the leak, please?

**Exercise 2 page 102**

1. b  2. a  3. b  4. a  5. b  6. b

**Exercise 3 page 103**

1. Could you fix the window, please?
2. Would you repair the refrigerator, please?
3. Can you fix the light, please?
4. Will you unclog the sink, please?
5. Could you change the lock, please?
6. Would you fix the dishwasher, please?

**Exercise 4 page 103**

1. Could you fix the light, please?
2. Could you unclog the bathtub, please?
3. Could you change the lightbulb, please?
4. Could you repair the dishwasher, please?
5. Could you clean the bathroom, please?
6. Could you call a plumber, please?

### Lesson D: Reading

**Exercise 1 page 104**

1. b  2. b  3. a  4. c  5. b  6. a

**Exercise 2 page 105**

1. burned out     6. jammed
2. broken         7. torn
3. dripping       8. scratched
4. bent           9. stained
5. cracked

**Exercise 3 page 105**

1. jammed         5. torn
2. broken         6. cracked
3. burned out     7. bent
4. dripping       8. scratched

### Lesson E: Writing

**Exercise 1 page 106**

1. broken         5. burned out
2. cracked        6. dripping
3. stained        7. scratched
4. jammed         8. clogged

**Exercise 2 page 106**

1. Three signatures.
2. 201, 412, 605, 822
3. December 2, 2009
4. Ms. Torrant
5. Sincerely
6. Three paragraphs.
7. Jim Bowen

**Exercise 3 page 107**

1. cracked bathtub
2. dishwasher
3. leaking
4. clogged toilet
5. stove
6. broken
7. carpet
8. stained

### Lesson F: Another view

**Exercise 1 page 108**

1. c  2. a  3. c  4. b  5. b  6. d

**Exercise 2 page 109**

1. a plumber
2. a stained carpet
3. burned-out lights
4. a locksmith
5. a plumber
6. a leaking sink
7. a broken lock
8. a painter
9. an appliance repair person
10. a carpenter

**Exercise 3 page 109**

1. bent key
2. clogged sink
3. burned-out lightbulb
4. jammed window
5. dripping faucet
6. stained carpet
7. broken lock
8. cracked window

## Unit 10: Leisure

### Lesson A: Get ready

**Exercise 1 page 110**

1. balloons
2. a piece of cake
3. a cake
4. perfume
5. flowers
6. a card
7. a present
8. a guest

**Exercise 2 page 110**

**Exercise 3 page 111**

1. b     5. a
2. a     6. c
3. b     7. c
4. a     8. b

### Lesson B: Would you like some cake?

**Exercise 1 page 112**

1. Would you like some cake?
2. Would they like some coffee?
3. Would you like some ice cream?
4. Would she like a balloon?
5. Would they like some flowers?
6. Would you like some dessert?
7. Would he like a cup of tea?

**Exercise 2 page 112**

1. a   3. a   5. a   7. b
2. b   4. b   6. a   8. b

**Exercise 3** page 113

1. They'd like some soda.
2. He'd like some coffee.
3. We'd like some salad.
4. she'd like a hot dog.
5. I'd like some fruit.
6. I'd like some cheese.

**Exercise 4** page 113

1. What would you
2. I'd like
3. Would you like
4. thanks
5. Would you like
6. please
7. Would you like
8. I'd like
9. Would you like
10. I'd like
11. What would they

**Lesson C: Tim gave Mary a present.**

**Exercise 1** page 114

1. Tim gave Mary a present.
2. Jim brought Sarah some flowers.
3. Elias wrote his father an e-mail.
4. Marta bought her son some soda.
5. Felix gave his children some ice cream.
6. Liu Na sent her mother a birthday card.

**Exercise 2** page 114

1. Tim gave her a present.
2. Jim brought her some flowers.
3. Elias wrote him an e-mail.
4. Marta bought him some soda.
5. Felix gave them some ice cream.
6. Liu Na sent her a birthday card.

**Exercise 3** page 115

1. barbecue grill
2. a salad bowl
3. linens
4. coffee cups
5. a check

**Exercise 4** page 115

1. Mina's parents gave them a check.
2. Penny gave them coffee cups.

3. Maria gave them a salad bowl.
4. Mina's sister gave them towels.
5. Mina sent them thank-you notes.

**Lesson D: Reading**

**Exercise 1** page 116

1. Halloween.
2. Last night.
3. The children.
4. Do-Cheon.
5. Stayed home and gave out candy.
6. About a month.

**Exercise 2** page 116

1. A wedding.
2. Thanksgiving.
3. Halloween.
4. Mother's Day.
5. New Year's Eve.
6. A baby shower.

**Exercise 3** page 117

1. d      6. h
2. a      7. c
3. i      8. f
4. g      9. e
5. b

**Exercise 4** page 117

**Parties**
a baby shower
a housewarming
New Year's Eve
a wedding

**No school or work**
Independence Day
Thanksgiving

**Give presents or cards**
a baby shower
a housewarming
Mother's Day
Valentine's Day
a wedding

**Lesson E: Writing**

**Exercise 1** page 118

1. Thank you for the interesting book you gave me.
2. I'm really excited about reading it.
3. Thank you for bringing a cake to our party.
4. I really liked it a lot.

5. Thank you for coming to my graduation party.
6. I hope you had a good time.

**Exercise 2** page 118

1. Thank you for the interesting book you gave me.
2. I'm really excited about reading it.
3. thank you for bringing a cake to our party.
4. I really liked it a lot.
5. Thank you for coming to my graduation party.
6. I hope you had a good time.

**Exercise 3** page 119

1. It was Joe's party.
2. He wrote it on June 15, 2009.
3. He wrote it to Erica.
4. Erica gave him a book.
5. Erica brought a chocolate cake to the party.
6. Joe liked the cake because chocolate is his favorite kind of cake.

**Exercise 4** page 119

1. Dan
2. chocolates
3. Valentine's Day
4. favorite
5. Thank you
6. hope

**Lesson F: Another view**

**Exercise 1** page 120

1. a      5. c
2. c      6. d
3. a      7. a
4. b      8. a

**Exercise 2** page 121

A, C, D, E, G, I

**Exercise 3** page 121

G. a baby shower
I. a birthday party
A. a graduation
E. Halloween
C. Independence Day
D. a wedding

## Illustration credits

**John Batten**: 14, 19, 26, 37, 69, 100

**Mona Daly**: 2, 9, 29, 62, 63, 86, 104

**Chuck Gonzales**: 27, 34, 38, 75, 87, 103

**Ben Hasler**: 20, 76

**Pamela Hobbs**: 4, 12, 32, 121

**Peter Hoey**: 25, 49, 81, 112

**Frank Montagna**: 5, 13, 51, 71, 88, 110

**Vilma Ortiz-Dillon**: 7, 16, 28, 45, 50, 51, 66, 73, 79, 98

## Photography credits

**3** (*clockwise from top left*) ©Jupiter Images; ©Jupiter Images; ©Inmagine; ©Shutterstock

**13** (*clockwise from top left*) ©Shutterstock; ©Inmagine; ©Jupiter Images; ©Jupiter Images; ©Jupiter Images; ©Alamy; ©Jupiter Images; ©Shutterstock

**15** ©Jupiter Images

**17** (*top to bottom*) ©Jupiter Images; ©Shutterstock; ©Shutterstock; ©Shutterstock

**21** (*clockwise from top left*) ©Inmagine; ©Punchstock; ©Shutterstock; ©Shutterstock; ©Inmagine; ©Inmagine; ©Inmagine; ©Inmagine

**22** ©Inmagine

**23** ©Inmagine

**35** (*top to bottom*) ©Jim Erickson/Jupiter Images; ©Jupiter Images

**39** (*left to right*) ©Inmagine; ©Inmagine; ©Jupiter Images

**41** ©Inmagine

**43** ©Inmagine

**58** ©Inmagine

**59** ©Inmagine

**65** ©Inmagine

**74** (*top row, left to right*) ©Shutterstock; ©Inmagine; (*middle row, left to right*) ©Inmagine; ©Alamy; ©Inmagine; ©Inmagine; (*bottom row, left to right*) ©Photo Edit; ©George Kerrigan

**79** (*top row, left to right*) ©Inmagine; ©Shutterstock; ©Alamy; (*middle row, left to right*) ©Jupiter Images; ©Jupiter Images; ©Shutterstock; (*bottom row, left to right*) ©Jupiter Images; ©Inmagine; ©Jupiter Images

**80** ©Inmagine

**93** (*left, top to bottom*) ©Jupiter Images; ©Shutterstock; ©Inmagine; ©Inmagine; (*right, top to bottom*) ©Inmagine; ©Jupiter Images; ©Shutterstock; ©Inmagine

**95** (*clockwise from top left*) ©Jupiter Images; ©Shutterstock; ©Alamy; ©Inmagine; ©Shutterstock; ©Jupiter Images

**97** ©Inmagine

**99** (*clockwise from top left*) ©Jupiter Images; ©Jupiter Images; ©Punchstock; ©Jupiter Images; ©Elizabeth Whiting & Associates/Corbis

**102** (*left to right*) ©Inmagine; ©Shutterstock; ©Mediacolor/Alamy

**113** (*clockwise from top left*) ©Shutterstock; ©Jupiter Images; ©Shutterstock; ©Jupiter Images; ©Jupiter Images; ©Shutterstock

**117** (*left to right*) ©Inmagine; ©Alamy; ©Inmagine